P9-CLR-369

Kids
– a Knitter's dozen

a production of **XRX** *BOOKS*

Kids; A Knitter's dozen PUBLISHED BY XRX BOOKS

Credits

PUBLISHER
Alexis Yiorgos Xenakis

COEDITORS
Rick Mondragon
Elaine Rowley

EDITORIAL ASSISTANT
Sue Kay Nelson

INSTRUCTION EDITOR
Joni Coniglio

INSTRUCTION ASSISTANTS
Kelly Rokke
Carol Thompson
Lizbeth Upitis

GRAPHIC DESIGNER
Bob Natz

PHOTOGRAPHER
Alexis Xenakis

SECOND PHOTOGRAPHER
Mike Winkleman

DIRECTOR, PUBLISHING SERVICES
David Xenakis

STYLISTS
Lisa Mannes
Rick Mondragon

TECHNICAL ILLUSTRATOR
Carol Skallerud

PRODUCTION DIRECTOR & COLOR SPECIALIST
Dennis Pearson

BOOK PRODUCTION MANAGER
Greg Hoogeveen

DIGITAL PREPRESS
Everett Baker
Nancy Holzer
Jay Reeve

MIS
Jason Bittner

FIRST PUBLISHED IN USA IN 2006 BY XRX, INC.

COPYRIGHT © 2006 XRX, INC.

All rights reserved.
No part of this publication may be reproduced, stored in a retrieval system,
or transmitted, in any form or by any means, electronic, mechanical,
photocopying, recording or otherwise, without the prior permission of the
copyright holder.

We give permission to readers to photocopy the instructions and graphics
for personal use only.

ISBN 1-933064-03-X
Produced in Sioux Falls, South Dakota, by XRX, Inc.,
PO Box 1525, Sioux Falls, SD 57101-1525 USA 605.338.2450

a publication of XRX BOOKS

Visit us online at knittinguniverse.com

Kids

–a Knitter's dozen

**photography by
Alexis Xenakis**

3

Flower Power

5

Ted & Sam

4

Colorful Combs

6

Button Me

2

Jester Stripes

1

Top-Down
Raglans

12

Celebration
Pullover

11

Pockets For Two

13

Danish Nursery
Jacket

14

Activity Sweater

15

Knitted Knotted

iv

Kids - a Knitter's dozen CONTENTS

Techniques
p 80

Specifications
p 86

1 2 **3** 4 5 6

At a Glance
p 87

v

R for Ryan
M for Maddy
S for Spencer

There's room in every child's
life for handshaped cookies
and handknit sweaters.

Let's keep it that way.

Go to
knittinguniverse.com
for a free download of our
Koulourakia recipe.

WELCOME

It's a bit like being a grandparent.

When we knit for a child, we don't have to deal with everyday parental concerns. We can be a bit indulgent, even a bit irresponsible. We can choose an impractical color. We can take time, spend a little extra on the yarn; after all, it's a small knit.

We know, and the child knows, that this is something special, something made just for her or for him.

We're knitting memories.

Throughout this book, the yarns are described generically and the specific yarn is listed with each photograph. Some of the yarns are no longer available, but may live on in our memories and stashes.

Corbin can't wait to wear his older sister's sweater. Fit will come later.

1a
Top-Down
Raglans
1b

EASY +

LOOSE FIT

2 (4/6, 8/10)
A 28 (33, 36)"
B 15½ (17½, 20½)"
C 17¼ (20¼, 22)"

10cm/4"

24, 30
18, 22

• over stockinette stitch (knit all rounds)
using larger needles

1 2 3 **4** 5 6

• Medium weight
• 300 (400, 500) yds

1 2 **3** 4 5 6

• Light weight
MC • 480 (630, 805) yds
A & B • 70 (95, 115) yds each

• 4mm/US6 and 5mm/US8, or size to obtain
gauge, 40 and 60cm/16" and 24" long
• 3.5mm/US4 and 4mm/US6,
or size to obtain gauge, 40 and 60cm/16"
and 24" long

• four 4mm/US6 and 5mm/US8
• four 3.5mm/US4 and 4mm/US6

4

OK, let's just say it. The best pullover to make for a child is a top-down raglan. Knit circularly, it couldn't be easier. A loop cast-on avoids Too-tight Neck—that instant turn-off for kids. And no neck shaping means our easy-on version can be worn either way—there is no real front or back.

Knitter's Design Team

Top-Down Raglans

it's easy ...go for it!

Notes

1 See *Techniques*, page 80, for Make 1 (M1), SSK, and loop cast-on. **2** Sweater is worked circularly from the neck down. **3** Use loop cast-on throughout. **4** Change to circular needles (on yoke) or dpns (on sleeves) as necessary. **5** Numbers for Version 1 appear first (in green) and numbers for Version 2 appear second (in black).

EASY-ON RAGLAN

Yoke

With smaller double-pointed needles (dpns) and MC (for Version 2), cast on 68 (72, 80) or 84 (88, 96) stitches. Place marker (pm) for beginning of round, join, and work in rounds of k2, p2 rib for ¾". Change to larger dpns.
Next round Knit, pm after every 17 (18, 20) or 21 (22, 24) stitches.
(***Note*** For Version 2, begin working Stripe Pattern for Yoke Chart.)
Increase round * K1, work open M1 (see box) or M1L, knit to 1 stitch before marker, work open M1 or M1R, k1; repeat from * 3 times more—76 (80, 88) or 92 (96, 104) stitches; 19 (20, 22) or 23 (24,

26) stitches between markers. Continue to increase 1 stitch each side of markers every round 9 (12, 13) or 11 (14, 16) times more, then every other round 11 (13, 14) or 14 (16, 17) times—236 (280, 304) or 292 (336, 368) stitches; 59 (70, 76) or 73 (84, 92) stitches between markers. Continue with MC only (for Version 2).

Divide for Body and Sleeves

Next round * Knit to marker, remove marker, place next 59 (70, 76) or 73 (84, 92) stitches on hold for sleeve, cast on 4 (4, 5) or 4 (6, 7) stitches for underarm, remove marker; repeat from * once more, placing a marker in center of cast-on underarm stitches for beginning of round—126 (148, 162) or 154 (180, 198) stitches.

Body

Work even for 7 (8, 10)".
Next round Knit, decreasing 6 (8, 10) or 10 (12, 14) stitches evenly around—120 (140, 152) or 144 (168, 184) stitches. Change to smaller circular needle and work in k2, p2 rib for 1¼". Bind off.

&
• stitch markers

Size 4/6 Version 1 (page 4-5, blue sweater) PLYMOUTH YARNS Jelli Beans (acrylic, wool; 50g; 107 yds) in 133
Version 2 (page 6-8) ROWAN Felted Tweed (wool; 50g; 191 yds) in 141 (MC), 146 (A), 143 (B)

Sleeves

With larger 16" circular needle and MC (Version 2), beginning at center of cast-on underarm stitches, pick up and knit 1 stitch in last 2 (2, 3) or 2 (3, 4) underarm stitches at one side of body, then knit 59 (70, 76) or 73 (84, 92) sleeve stitches from holder, then pick up and knit 1 stitch in remaining 2 or 2 (3, 3) cast-on underarm stitches—63 (74, 81) or 77 (90, 99) stitches. Pm for beginning of round, join, and knit 1 round, decreasing 1 (0, 1) stitch—62 (74, 80) or 76 (90, 98) stitches.

Knit 1 round.

Decrease round K1, SSK, knit to last 3 stitches, k2tog, k1.

Knit 2 rounds.

Repeat from* 16 (20, 21) or 19 (24, 26) times more—28 (32, 36) or 36 (40, 44) stitches.

Change to smaller dpns and work 2" in k2, p2 rib. Bind off loosely.

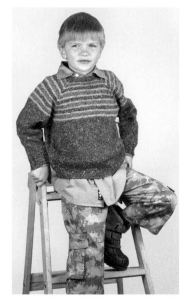

OPEN MAKE 1

1 Insert left needle from front to back under strand between last stitch knitted and first stitch on left needle. Knit this strand.

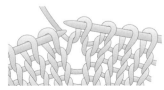

2 Completed Open M1: a non-twisted increase.

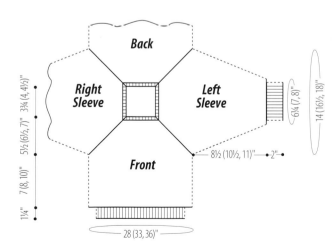

Back

Right Sleeve

Left Sleeve

Front

3¾ (4, 4½)"
5½ (6½, 7)"
7 (8, 10)"
1¼"
6¼ (7, 8)"
14 (16½, 18)"
8½ (10½, 11)" — 2"
28 (33, 36)"

Stripe Pattern for Yoke Chart

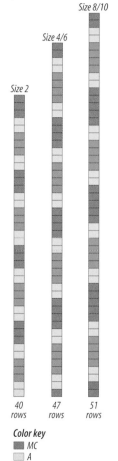

Size 8/10

Size 4/6

Size 2

40 rows

47 rows

51 rows

Color key
MC
A
B

5

Top-down Raglans

Neck shaping refines the fit of our top-down raglan. It's circular construction allows the fit to be checked and adjusted as it grows. Just slip stitches on a thread and try it on.

Knitter's Design Team

INTERMEDIATE

STANDARD FIT

2 (4, 6, 8, 10, 12)
A 24 (26, 28, 30, 32, 34)"
B 14½ (15½, 16¼, 17½, 19, 20¼)"
C 15½ (17, 18¼, 19¾, 20¼, 21½)"

10cm/4"

28 ▦ 20

• over stockinette stitch (knit all rounds), using larger needles

1 2 3 **4** 5 6

• Medium weight
A • 40 (40, 45, 45, 50, 50) yds
B • 60 (70, 85, 95, 105, 125) yds
C • 135 (140, 155, 165, 175, 185) yds
D • 110 (140, 165, 210, 250, 295) yds

• 3.75mm/US5 and 4.5mm/US7,
or size to obtain gauge, 40 and 60cm/16"
and 24" long

• four 3.75mm/US5 and 4.5mm/US7

&

• stitch markers

Notes
1 See *Techniques*, page 80, for Make 1 (M1), SSK, and loop cast-on. *2* Sweater is worked circularly from the neck down. *3* Use loop cast-on throughout. *4* Change to longer circular needle (on yoke) or double-point needles (dpns) (on sleeves) as necessary. *5* Slip stitches purlwise with yarn at WS of work.

Hide Knit Wrap (HKW) Knit stitch and short-row wrap together.

Hide Purl Wrap (HPW) Purl stitch and short-row wrap together.

HPW (on a knit row) Slip wrap and stitch together knitwise to right needle (illustration 1), then insert left needle into the stitches (illustration 2) and knit them together.

SHAPED-NECK RAGLAN
Yoke
With A, cast on 64 (68, 76, 80, 88, 92) stitches divided over 3 dpns. Place marker (pm) for beginning of round, join, and work in rounds of k2, p2 rib for 1¼".

Change to larger 16" circular needle and B. *Next round* Knit, pm after 12 (12, 14, 14, 16, 16) stitches, another after 20 (22, 24, 26, 28, 30) stitches, and another after 12 (12, 14, 14, 16, 16) stitches, knit to 1 stitch before round marker (left front raglan).
Begin short-row neck shaping: Row 1 (RS) *M1R, k1, slip marker (sm), k1, M1L, knit to 1 stitch before marker; repeat from* twice more, M1R, k1, sm (right front raglan), k1, M1L, wrap next stitch and turn (W&T). *Row 2* (WS) Slip 1, purl to 4th marker, sm, p2, W&T. *Row 3* Slip 1, M1R, k1, sm, k1, M1L, *knit to 1 stitch before marker, M1R, k1, sm, k1, M1L; repeat from* twice more, k1, HKW, W&T. *Row 4* Slip 1, purl to 4th marker, sm, p3, HPW, W&T. *Row 5* Slip 1, *knit to 1 stitch before marker, M1R, k1, sm, k1, M1L; repeat from* 3 times more, k3, HKW, W&T. *Row 6* Repeat Row 4, end p5, HPW, W&T. *Row 7* Repeat Row 5, end k5, HKW, W&T. *Row 8* Repeat Row 4, end p7, HPW, W&T. *Row 9* Repeat Row 5, end k7, HKW, W&T. *Row 10* Repeat Row 4, end p9, HPW, W&T.
Sizes 8, 10 and 12 only: Row 11 Repeat Row 5, end k9, HKW, W&T. *Row 12* Repeat Row 4, end p11, HPW, W&T.

Size 10 NASHUA Creative Focus Worsted (wool, alpaca; 100g; 220 yds) in 3864 (A), 1180 (B), 2190 (C), 3729 (D)

REFINED SHORT ROWS

Each short row adds 2 rows of knitting across a section of the work. Since the work is turned before completing a row, stitches must be wrapped at the turn to prevent holes. Wrap and turn as follows:

Knit side

1 With yarn in back, slip next stitch as if to purl. Bring yarn to front of work and slip stitch back to left needle (as shown). Turn work.

2 With yarn in front, slip next stitch as if to purl. Work to end.

3 When you come to the wrap on a following knit row, hide the wrap by knitting it together with the stitch it wraps (HKW).

The first stitch of each short row is slipped (Step 2); this tapers the ends of short rows. When the wraps are hidden (Step 3), the mechanics of the shaping are almost invisible.

Purl side

1 With yarn in front, slip next stitch as if to purl. Bring yarn to back of work and slip stitch back to left needle (as shown). Turn work.

2 With yarn in back, slip next stitch as if to purl. Work to end.

3 When you come to the wrap on a following purl row, hide the wrap by purling it together with the stitch it wraps (HPW).

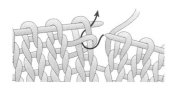 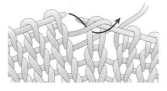

HPW on a knit row

1 Slip wrap and stitch together knitwise to right needle.

2 Insert left needle into the stitches and knit them together.

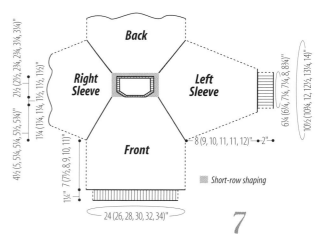

Back

Right Sleeve

Left Sleeve

Front

2½ (2½, 2¾, 2¾, 3¼, 3¼)"

1¼ (1¼, 1¼, 1½, 1½, 1½)"

4½ (5, 5¼, 5¼, 5½, 5¾)"

6¼ (6¼, 7¼, 7¼, 8, 8¾)"

10¼ (10¾, 12, 12½, 13¾, 14)"

1½" 7 (7½, 8, 9, 10, 11)"

8 (9, 10, 11, 11, 12)"—•–2"•

■ Short-row shaping

1½" 7 (7½, 8, 9, 10, 11)"

24 (26, 28, 30, 32, 34)"

7

All sizes: Next round (RS) Slip 1, *knit to 1 stitch before marker, M1R, k1, sm, k1, M1L; repeat from* 3 times more, k9 (9, 9, 11, 11, 11), HKW, k8 (10, 12, 12, 14, 16), HPW (on knit row), knit to marker—112 (116, 124, 136, 144, 148) stitches.
Next round Knit to 1 stitch before round marker. **Increase round** *M1R, k1, sm, k1, M1L, knit to 1 stitch before marker; repeat from* 3 times more, end k1—120 (124, 132, 144, 152, 156) stitches. Repeat last 2 rounds 11 (12, 13, 13, 14, 15) times more—208 (220, 236, 248, 264, 276) stitches. Knit 1 round. Change to A and knit 2 rounds. Change to C.

Divide for body and sleeves

Next round *Remove marker, place next 48 (50, 54, 56, 60, 62) stitches on hold for sleeve, remove marker, cast on 4 (5, 6, 7, 8, 9) stitches for underarm, knit to marker; repeat from* once more, knitting to end of front—120 (130, 140, 150, 160, 170) stitches.

Body

Next round Join. K2 (2, 3, 3, 4, 4), place marker for beginning of round, knit to end of round. Work even for 33 rounds. Work 2 rounds with A. Change to D and work even until body measures 7 (7½, 8, 9, 10, 11)" from underarm. Change to A.
Next round Knit, decreasing 0 (2, 0, 2, 0, 2) stitches—120 (128, 140, 148, 160, 168) stitches.

Change to smaller circular needle and work in k2, p2 rib for 1¼". Bind off.

Sleeves

With larger 16" circular needle and C, beginning at center of cast-on underarm stitches, pick up and knit 1 stitch in each of last 2 (3, 3, 4, 4, 5) underarm stitches at one side of body, then knit sleeve stitches from holder, then pick up and knit 1 stitch in each of remaining 2 (2, 3, 3, 4, 4) underarm stitches—52 (55, 60, 63, 68, 71) stitches. Pm for beginning of round, join, and knit 1 round, decreasing 0 (1, 0, 1, 0, 1) stitch—52 (54, 60, 62, 68, 70) stitches. Knit 1 round.
Decrease round K1, SSK, knit to last 3 stitches, k2tog, k1. Knit 2 rounds. Repeat from* 9 (10, 11, 12, 13, 12) times more, AT SAME TIME, after 34 rounds of C have been worked, work 2 rounds A, then continue with D—32 (32, 36, 36, 40, 44) stitches.
Change to A and knit 1 round. Change to smaller dpns and work in k2, p2 rib for 2". Bind off loosely.

Jester
Stripes

2

Your little one will be ever so cute in this jester stripe top and matching scarf. Seed stitch patterning on the tabs and color changes add depth to the vertical stripes in the easy, side-to-side sweater.

Designed by Katharine Hunt

Jester Stripes

INTERMEDIATE +

LOOSE FIT

6 (8, 10, 12)
A 29½ (32, 33, 36)"
B 16½ (17½, 18¾, 20)"
C 19 (20, 22, 23)"
SCARF 5½ x 44½"

10cm/4"

24, 31

18, 17

• over stockinette stitch (knit on RS, purl on WS), using larger needles
• over seed stitch, using smaller needles

1 2 3 **4** 5 6

• Medium weight
A • 205 (200, 230, 280) yds
B • 165 (210, 250, 240) yds
C • 135 (170, 185, 250) yds
D • 90 (95, 100, 110) yds
Scarf A, C • 70 yds
B • 65 yds
D • 35 yds

• 4.5mm/US7 and 5.5mm/US9, or size to obtain gauge

• 4.5mm/US7, 40cm/16" long

• stitch markers

Notes
1 See *Techniques*, page 80 for cable cast-on. **2** Body of sweater is worked from side to side in one piece.

Seed Stitch (odd number of stitches)
Row 1 *K1, p1; repeat from*, end k1. Repeat Row 1 for Seed Stitch.

Stripe Pattern for Body
Note (Follow Color Sequence Chart for size you are making.)
Row 1 (RS) [K1, p1] 3 times, knit to last 6 stitches, [p1, k1] 3 times.
Row 2 [K1, p1] twice, k1, purl to last 5 stitches, [k1, p1] twice, k1.
Row 3 [K1, p1] twice, knit to last 4 stitches, [p1, k1] twice.
Row 4 Repeat Row 2.
Row 5 Repeat Row 1.
Row 6 [K1, p1] 3 times, k1, purl to last 7 stitches, [k1, p1] 3 times, k1.
Row 7 [K1, p1] 4 times, knit to last 8 stitches, [p1, k1] 4 times.
Row 8 Bind off 3 stitches, *k1, p1; repeat from*, end k1.
Row 9 Bind off 3 stitches, slip remaining stitch on right needle to left needle, cut yarn, join new color, *p1, k1; repeat from*, end p1, cable cast on 3 stitches.
Row 10 *K1, p1; repeat from* to end, cable cast on 3 stitches.
Row 11 Repeat Row 7.
Row 12 Repeat Row 6. Repeat Rows 1–12 for Stripe Pattern for Body.

PULLOVER
Body
Shape left side
With larger needles and A (A, A, C), cast on 149 (159, 169, 181) stitches. Begin with pattern row 1 (3, 1, 3), work Stripe Pattern for Body, following Color Sequence Chart (for size you are making) for color changes, for 25 (27, 29, 33) rows, ending with pattern row 1 (5, 5, 11) of stripe D. Mark 75th (80th, 85th, 91st) stitch (for center).
Shape neck
Next row (WS) Work 68 (73, 78, 83) stitches, join 2nd ball of yarn and bind off 7 (7, 7, 8) stitches, work to end. Working both sides at same time, decrease 1 stitch at each neck edge every row 3 times, then continue to decrease 1 stitch at front neck edge only every row 3 times more—71 (76, 81, 87)

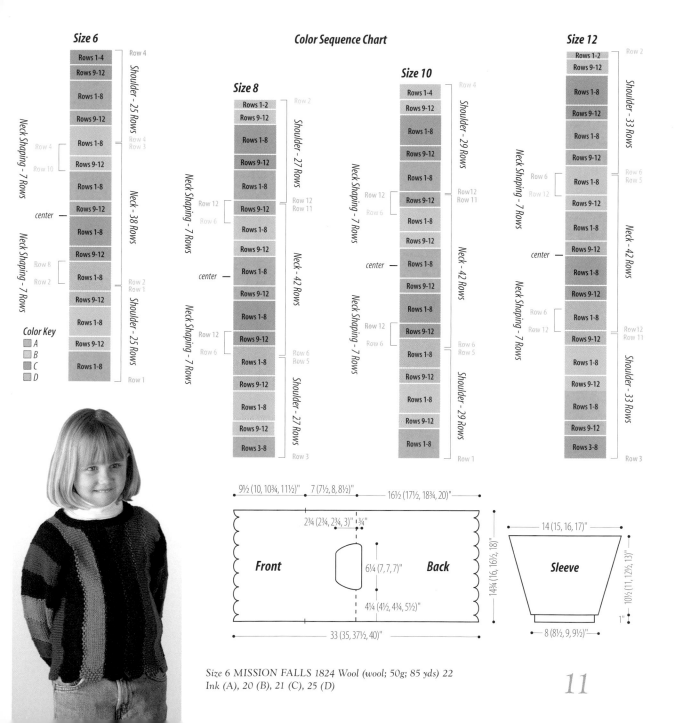

Color Sequence Chart

Size 6

Rows 1-4	Row 4
Rows 9-12	
Rows 1-8	Shoulder - 25 Rows
Rows 9-12	Row 4 / Row 3
Rows 1-8	
Rows 9-12	
Rows 1-8	
Rows 9-12	Neck - 38 Rows
Rows 1-8	
Rows 9-12	
Rows 1-8	Row 2 / Row 1
Rows 9-12	
Rows 1-8	Shoulder - 25 Rows
Rows 9-12	
Rows 1-8	Row 1

Neck Shaping - 7 Rows (Row 4 / Row 10)
center
Neck Shaping - 7 Rows (Row 8 / Row 2)

Color Key
- A
- B
- C
- D

Size 8

Rows 1-2	Row 2
Rows 9-12	
Rows 1-8	Shoulder - 27 Rows
Rows 9-12	
Rows 1-8	
Rows 9-12	Row 12 / Row 11
Rows 1-8	
Rows 9-12	
Rows 1-8	
Rows 9-12	Neck - 42 Rows
Rows 1-8	
Rows 9-12	
Rows 1-8	Row 6 / Row 5
Rows 9-12	
Rows 1-8	Shoulder - 27 Rows
Rows 9-12	
Rows 3-8	Row 3

Neck Shaping - 7 Rows (Row 12 / Row 6)
center
Neck Shaping - 7 Rows (Row 12 / Row 6)

Size 10

Rows 1-4	Row 4
Rows 9-12	
Rows 1-8	Shoulder - 29 Rows
Rows 9-12	
Rows 1-8	
Rows 9-12	Row 12 / Row 11
Rows 1-8	
Rows 9-12	
Rows 1-8	
Rows 9-12	Neck - 42 Rows
Rows 1-8	
Rows 9-12	
Rows 1-8	Row 6 / Row 5
Rows 9-12	
Rows 1-8	Shoulder - 29 Rows
Rows 9-12	
Rows 1-8	Row 1

Neck Shaping - 7 Rows (Row 12 / Row 6)
center
Neck Shaping - 7 Rows (Row 12 / Row 6)

Size 12

Rows 1-2	Row 2
Rows 9-12	
Rows 1-8	Shoulder - 33 Rows
Rows 9-12	
Rows 1-8	
Rows 9-12	Row 6 / Row 5
Rows 1-8	
Rows 9-12	
Rows 1-8	Neck - 42 Rows
Rows 9-12	
Rows 1-8	
Rows 9-12	Row 12 / Row 11
Rows 1-8	
Rows 9-12	Shoulder - 33 Rows
Rows 1-8	
Rows 9-12	
Rows 3-8	Row 3

Neck Shaping - 7 Rows (Row 6 / Row 12)
center
Neck Shaping - 7 Rows (Row 6 / Row 12)

Front / **Back**

9½ (10, 10¾, 11½)" 7 (7½, 8, 8½)" 16½ (17½, 18¾, 20)"
2¾ (2¾, 2¾, 3)" 1¾"
6¼ (7, 7, 7)"
4¼ (4½, 4¾, 5½)"
14¾ (16, 16½, 18)"
33 (35, 37½, 40)"

Sleeve

14 (15, 16, 17)"
10½ (11, 12½, 13)"
1"
8 (8½, 9, 9½)"

Size 6 MISSION FALLS 1824 Wool (wool; 50g; 85 yds) 22
Ink (A), 20 (B), 21 (C), 25 (D)

11

stitches on back, and 62 (67, 72, 77) stitches on front. Work 25 (29, 29, 29) rows even. Increase 1 stitch at front neck edge every row 3 times, then increase 1 stitch at both neck edges every row 3 times.

Shape right side

Next row (WS) Work to end of first half, cast on 7 (7, 7, 8) stitches, then work to end of 2nd half—149 (159, 169, 181) stitches. Work even to end of Color Sequence Chart. Bind off.

Left Sleeve

With smaller needles and A (A, C, A), cast on 37 (39, 41, 43) stitches.
Begin Seed Stitch: Row 1 (RS) *K1, p1; repeat from*, end k1.
Rows 2–6 Repeat Row 1. Change to larger needles. Work Stripe Pattern Chart for Left Sleeve, AT SAME TIME, increase 1 stitch each side (working increases into pattern) on 3rd row, then every 4th row 9 (14, 12, 14) times, every 6th row 3 (0, 3, 2) times—63 (69, 73, 77) stitches. Work even through chart row 64 (66, 76, 78). Mark 32nd (35th, 37th, 39th) stitch (for center). Bind off.

Right Sleeve

With smaller needles and B (B, A, B), cast on 37 (39, 41, 43) stitches. Work as for left sleeve, following Stripe Pattern Chart for Right Sleeve.

Finishing

Block pieces.
Neckband
With RS facing, circular needle and A, begin at left shoulder and pick up and k77 (85, 85, 87) stitches evenly around neck edge. Place marker, join, and work Seed Stitch in rounds as follows:
Round 1 *K1, p1; repeat from*, end k1.
Round 2 *P1, k1; repeat from*, end p1. Repeat Rounds 1 and 2 once more, then work Round 1 once more. Bind off.
Sew sleeves to body, matching center stitch markers and colors. Sew side and sleeve seams.

SCARF

With smaller needles and A, cast on 189 stitches. **Begin Seed Stitch and Stripe Pattern: Rows 1–5** Work in Seed Stitch.
Row 6 Bind off 3 stitches, work to end.
Row 7 Bind off 3 stitches with A, slip stitch from right needle to left needle, cut A, join C and work in pattern to end, cable cast on 3 stitches.
Row 8 Work in pattern to end, cable cast on 3 stitches.
Rows 9–11 Work in Seed Stitch.
Row 12 Bind off 3 stitches, work to end. Repeat Rows 7–12, working stripes as follows: 6 rows each with B, A, D, and B. With C, work Rows 7–11 once more. Work 1 row Seed Stitch. Bind off.

Sleeve Stripe Pattern Chart

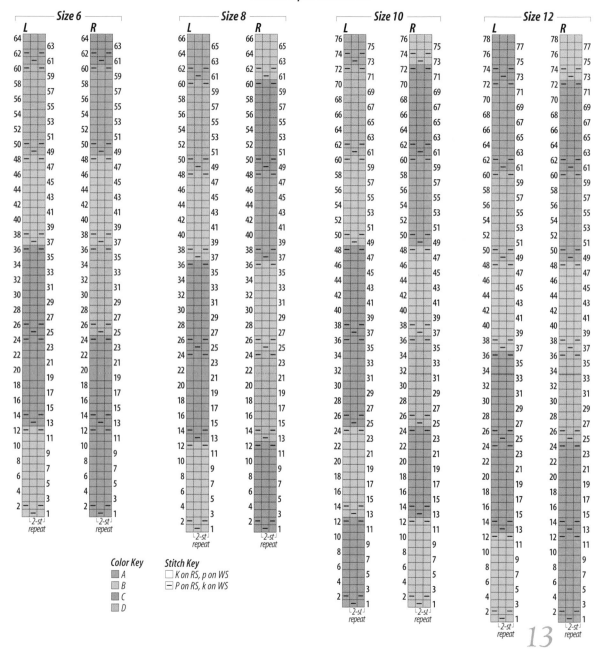

Color Key
- A
- B
- C
- D

Stitch Key
- ☐ K on RS, p on WS
- ⊟ P on RS, k on WS

13

Stripes are always fun, and colors that cover half the spectrum can straddle a child's wardrobe easily. I-cord flower accents can be added or not.

3

Designed by Uschi Nolte

Flower Power

Note
See *Techniques*, page 80, for I-cord.

Stripe Pattern
Work in stockinette stitch (St st) as follows: *6 rows B, 6 rows C, 1 row D, 6 rows A; repeat from* (19 rows) for Stripe Pattern.

Notes on working Stripe Pattern
Carry yarn along side of work until you need it again. To avoid long strands, catch the yarn once around the working yarn of another color. Because color D is worked over only one row, the yarn will change sides every time it is used. To avoid having to cut and rejoin yarns, work with a circular needle so you can slide work to whichever end of needle is necessary to pick up correct color. This will mean occasionally working 2 consecutive RS or WS rows.

Back
With larger needles and A, cast on 80 (86, 92, 98) stitches. Work in St st for 8 rows. Work in Stripe Pattern until piece measures 7½ (9, 10, 10)" from beginning (with edge rolled), end with a WS row. Place markers each side for beginning of armholes. Work even until armhole measures 6½ (7, 7, 7½)" above markers. Bind off.

Front
Work as for back until armhole measures 4 (4½, 4½, 5)" above markers, end with a WS row.
Shape neck
Next row (RS) Work 34 (37, 38, 41) stitches, join 2nd ball of yarn and bind off center 12 (12, 16, 16) stitches, work to end. Working both sides at same time, bind off from each neck edge 2 stitches twice, then decrease 1 stitch each side every RS row 4 times—26 (29, 30, 33) stitches each side. Work even until piece measures same length as back to shoulders. Bind off.

Size 10 LANA GROSSA Numero Uno in 12 (A), 87 (B), 94 (C), and 92 (D)

INTERMEDIATE

C
B [A]
LOOSE FIT
4 (6, 8, 10)
A 28 (30, 32, 34)"
B 14 (16, 17, 17½)"
C 18 (19, 20, 21)"

10cm/4"
32 ▦
23
• over stockinette stitch (knit on RS, purl on WS) using larger needles

1 2 **3** 4 5 6
• Light weight
A • 240 (285, 315, 345) yds
B, C • 185 (225, 250, 275) yds
D • 70 (75, 80, 85) yds

• 4.5mm/US7, or size to obtain gauge
74cm/29" long
• 4mm/US6, 40cm/16" long

• two 4mm/US6

• stitch markers

Sleeves

With larger needles and A, cast on 36 (40, 40, 44) stitches. Work in St st for 8 rows. Work in Stripe Pattern, AT SAME TIME, increase 1 stitch each side every 4th row 19 (20, 18, 19) times, then every 6th row 0 (0, 2, 2) times—74 (80, 80, 86) stitches. Work even until piece measures 11 (11½, 12, 12½)" from beginning (with edge rolled). Bind off.

Finishing

Block pieces. Sew shoulders.
Neckband
With RS facing, smaller circular needle and A, begin at left shoulder and pick up and knit 72 (72, 80, 80) stitches evenly around neck edge. Place marker, join and knit 10 rounds. Bind off.
Sew top of sleeves between armhole markers. Sew side and sleeve seams.
Flowers (make 3)
With double-pointed needles and D, cast on 4 stitches. Work I-cord for 18". Bind off, leaving a long tail for sewing. Using template as a guide, sew cords in flower shape on front and back.

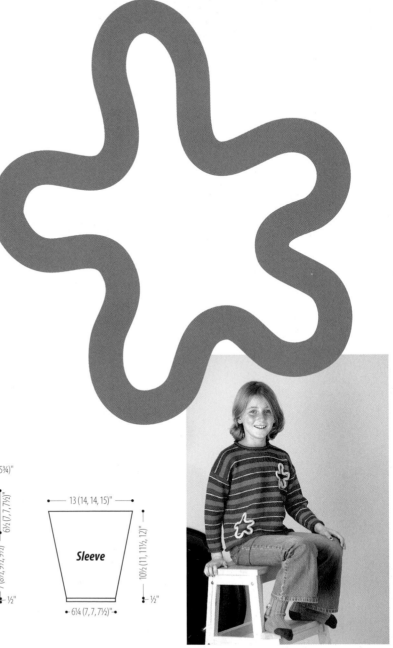

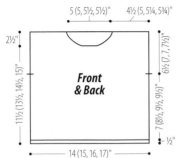

Front & Back

5 (5, 5½, 5½)"   4½ (5, 5¼, 5¾)"
2½"
11½ (13½, 14½, 15)"
6½ (7, 7, 7½)"
7 (8½, 9½, 9½)"
½"
14 (15, 16, 17)"

Sleeve

13 (14, 14, 15)"
10½ (11, 11½, 12)"
½"
6¼ (7, 7, 7½)"

16

Kids tend to like bright, energetic colors. These colors look like they've jumped from the crayon box onto this pullover. The repeating vertical and horizontal stripe design was inspired by a Peruvian chulla hat.

Designed by Kathy Zimmerman

Colorful Combs

INTERMEDIATE

LOOSE FIT
2/4 (6, 10, 12)
A 27½ (30½, 33½, 36½)"
B 14 (15, 16¼, 17½)"
C 17 (19½, 21, 22½)"

10cm/4"

28

26

• over Chart Pattern, using larger needles

1 2 **3** 4 5 6

• Light weight
MC • 330 (410, 475, 560) yds
A-E • 65 (85, 95, 115) yds each

• 3.75mm/US5 and 4.5mm/US7,
or size to obtain gauge

• 3.75mm/US5, 40cm/16" long

• stitch holders and marker

Note

See *Techniques*, page 80, for 3-needle bind-off.

Back

With smaller needles and MC, cast on 89 (99, 109, 119) stitches. Work in k1, p1 rib for 1", end with a WS row. Change to larger needles. Work in Chart Pattern until piece measures approximately 8¼ (8¼, 9½, 9½)" from beginning, end with chart row 10 (10, 18, 18).

Shape armholes

Bind off 10 (12, 14, 16) stitches at beginning of next 2 rows—69 (75, 81, 87) stitches. Work even until armhole measures approximately 4½ (5½, 5½, 6¾)", end with chart row 2 (10, 18, 26).

Shape neck

Next row (RS) Work 21 (23, 25, 27) stitches, join 2nd ball of yarn and bind off center 27 (29, 31, 33) stitches, work to end. Working both sides at same time, bind off from each neck edge 2 stitches 3 times—15 (17, 19, 21) stitches each side. Work 1 row even, ending with chart row 10 (18, 26, 34). Armhole measures approximately 5¾ (6¾, 6¾, 8)". Place stitches on hold.

Front

Work as for back until armhole measures approximately 3¼ (4¼, 4¼, 5½)", end with chart row 34 (2, 10, 18).

Shape neck

Next row (RS) Work 25 (27, 29, 31) stitches, join 2nd ball of yarn and bind off center 19 (21, 23, 25) stitches, work to end. Working both sides at same time, bind off from each neck edge 2 stitches 4 times, then decrease 1 stitch at each neck edge every RS row twice—15 (17, 19, 21) stitches each side. Work 3 rows even. Armhole measures same length as back to shoulder. Place stitches on hold.

Sleeves

With smaller needles and MC, cast on 43 (45, 49, 51) stitches. Work in k1, p1 rib for 1", end with a WS row. Change to larger needles. Work in Chart Pattern, increasing 1 stitch each side (working increases into pattern) on 3rd row, then every other row 0 (4, 0, 8) times, every 4th row 15 (16, 15, 17) times, every 6th row 0 (0, 3, 0) times—75 (87, 87, 103)

Size 6 PLYMOUTH Wildflower DK (cotton, acrylic; 50g; 137 yds) in 45 (MC), 46 (A), 56 (B), 48 (C), 11 (D), 55 (E)

stitches. Work 11 (15, 17, 19) rows even, ending with chart row 34 (10, 18, 26). Piece measures approximately 11½ (14, 15, 16)" from beginning. Bind off.

Finishing

Block pieces. Join shoulders, using 3-needle bind-off and MC.

Neckband

With RS facing, circular needle and MC, begin at left shoulder and pick up and knit 14 stitches along left front neck, 19 (21, 23, 25) stitches along center front neck, 14 stitches along right front neck, 6 stitches along right back neck, 27 (29, 31, 33) stitches along center back neck, and 6 stitches along left back neck—86 (90, 94, 98) stitches. Place marker, join and work in k1, p1 rib for 1". Bind off in rib.

Sew top of sleeves to straight edges of armholes. Sew straight portion at top of sleeves to bound-off armhole stitches. Sew side and sleeve seams.

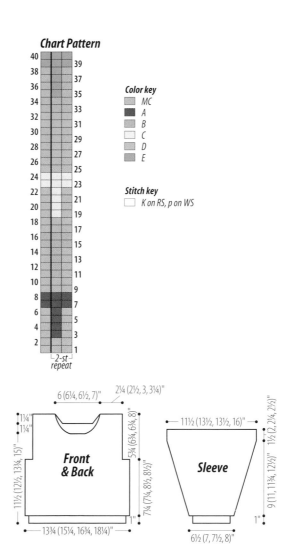

Chart Pattern

Color key
- MC
- A
- B
- C
- D
- E

Stitch key
- ☐ K on RS, p on WS

2-st repeat

6 (6¼, 6½, 7)"   2¼ (2½, 3, 3¼)"

1¼"
1¼"

11½ (12½, 13¾, 15)"

Front & Back

5¾ (6¾, 6¾, 8)"

7¼ (7¼, 8½, 8½)"

1"

13¾ (15¼, 16¾, 18¼)"

11½ (13½, 13½, 16)"

1½ (2, 2¼, 2½)"

Sleeve

9 (11, 11¾, 12½)"

1"

6½ (7, 7½, 8)"

'Odds to evens' placement yields interesting, rhythmic stripe designs. Two colors are used in a three-stripe sequence in these cardigans. They are worked in the round to explore steeks in a drop-shoulder design for Ted (the bear) and a set-in-sleeve option for Sam.

Designed by Rick Mondragon

Ted and Sam

INTERMEDIATE

STANDARD FIT

Child's sweater • 4 (6, 8, 10)
A 32 (34¼, 36½, 38¾)"
B 14 (15, 16, 17)"
C 19 (20½, 21½, 22)"
Bear's sweater • to fit 11" bear
A 14¼"
B 6"

10cm/4"

28

18

• over stockinette stitch (knit on RS, purl on WS) using larger needle

1 2 3 **4** 5 6

• Medium weight
A & B • 645 (725, 800, 870) yds each
(this will make both child's & bear's sweaters)

• 3.75mm/US5 and 4.5mm/US7, or size to obtain gauge, 40cm/16" (**bear's**) and 60cm/24" (**child's**) long

Notes
1 See *Techniques*, page 80, for SSK, crochet chain stitch, and loop cast-on. **2** Sweaters are worked circularly with steek stitches at center front and armholes. After pieces are complete, steek stitches are secured with crocheted chain, then cut and sewn. (See crochet-and-cut-steek illustration on page 21; for more on steeks, read *Steek Tricks* on page 24.) **3** Steek stitches are not included in stitch counts or measurements.

BEAR'S SWEATER
Body
With smaller 16" needle and A, cast on 51 stitches.
Begin rib pattern: Row 1 (RS) P1, *k1, p1; repeat from*. **Row 2** K1, *p1, k1; repeat from*. Repeat these 2 rows twice more. Change to larger 16" needle.
Next row (RS) Knit and increase 10 stitches evenly across—61 stitches. Do not turn. **Joining round** Place marker (pm) on needle for beginning of round, loop cast on 4 stitches (center front steek),

• four each 3.75mm/US5 and 4.5mm/US7

stitch markers

• 3.75mm/F

• five 19mm/¾" (child's)
• four 12mm/½" (bear's)

pm, then knit stitches from other end of needle around to round marker.
Begin Stripe Pattern: Round 1 With B, k1 through back loop (tbl), k2, k1 tbl, then knit to end of round. Continue in Stripe Pattern, following chart, and continue to knit first and last steek stitches tbl every round, until piece measures approximately 3½" from beginning, end with chart round 18.
Divide for underarm
Next round Work steek stitches, then k12 (right front), bind off 6 stitches (underarm), knit until there are 25 stitches (for back), bind off 6 stitches (underarm), knit to end (left front).
Next round *Work to bound-off underarm stitches, pm, loop cast on 4 stitches (armhole steek), pm; repeat from* once more, knit to end.
Next round *Work to armhole steek, work steek stitches as before; repeat from* once more, work to end.
Shape V-neck
Decrease round Work steek stitches, k1, k2tog, work to last 3 stitches of round, SSK, k1. Repeat decrease round every other round 4 times more—7 stitches for each front shoulder, 25 stitches for back. Work 6 rounds even. Armhole measures approximately 2½". Bind off.

Sleeves

With A, cast on 24 stitches divided over 3 smaller double-pointed needles (dpns). Join and work in k1, p1 rib for 6 rounds. Change to larger dpns. Knit 2 rounds with A, then work Stripe Pattern through chart round 18. Work next 4 chart rounds back and forth in stockinette stitch (purl on WS, knit on RS). Bind off.

Finishing

Block pieces. Secure steeks by working crochet chain stitch through every round of first and 4th stitch of steek. Cut through center of steeks. Sew shoulders. Set in sleeves.

Front and neck band

Place 4 markers along left front edge for buttonholes, with the first ½" above lower edge, the last at first V-neck decrease, and 2 others spaced evenly between. With RS facing, smaller needle and A, begin at lower edge and pick up and knit 22 stitches along right front edge to beginning of V-neck shaping, 12 stitches to shoulder, 11 stitches along back neck, 12 stitches along left front V-neck, and 22 stitches along left front edge—79 stitches. Work in k1, p1 rib for 5 rows, working buttonholes (yo, k2tog) at markers on 3rd row. Bind off. Whipstitch down crochet chain, while tucking ends under to neaten edges. Sew on buttons.

Bear's Stripe Pattern

Color key
- A
- B

Bear's Sweater

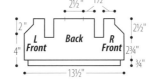

CROCHET-AND-CUT STEEK

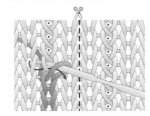

1 Prepare for the crochet steek by knitting the stitch before and after the center steek stitches through the back loop.

2 Holding yarn on the wrong side and crochet hook on the right side, chain through each twisted stitch in every round from bottom to top.

3 Cut through the center of the steek to form an opening.

USING STEEKS

1 A modified shoulder cardigan: The shaded areas are the steek stitches, x's are the decreased shaping for neck.

2 Secure both edges of each steek (front, armholes, and sleeves) with crochet chain stitch. See above for close-up.

3 Cut steeks to make openings.

4 Seam sleeves to body, work button band, neaten inside edges and wear.

21

48
47
46
45
44
43
42
41
40
39
38
37
36
35
34
33
32
31
30
29
28
27
26
25
24
23
22
21
20
19
18
17
16
15
14
13
12
11
10
9
8
7
6
5
4
3
2
1

Color key
☐ A
☐ B

CHILD'S SWEATER

Body

With smaller 24" needle and A, cast on 129 (139, 149, 159) stitches.

Begin rib pattern: Row 1 (RS) P1, *k1, p1; repeat from*.

Row 2 K1, *p1, k1; repeat from*. Repeat these 2 rows 4 times more. Change to larger 24" needle.

Next row (RS) Knit and increase 12 stitches evenly across—141 (151, 161, 171) stitches. Do not turn.

Joining round Place marker (pm) on needle for beginning of round, loop cast on 4 stitches (center front steek), pm, then knit stitches from other end of needle around to round marker.

Begin Stripe Pattern: Round 1 With B, k1 through back loop (tbl), k2, k1 tbl, then knit to end of round. Continue in Stripe Pattern, following chart, and continue to knit first and last steek stitches tbl every round, until piece measures approximately 9 (9¼, 9½, 10½)" from beginning, end with chart round 6 (8, 10, 16).

Divide for underarm

Next round Work steek stitches, then knit 32 (34, 36, 39) stitches (right front), bind off 8 stitches (underarm), knit until there are 61 (67, 73, 77) stitches (for back), bind off 8 stitches (underarm), knit to end (left front).

Next round *Work to bound-off underarm stitches, pm, loop cast on 4 stitches (armhole steek), pm; repeat from* once more, knit to end.

Shape armholes and V-neck

Armhole decrease round *Work to 3 stitches before armhole steek, SSK, k1, work steek stitches, k1, k2tog; repeat from* once more, work to end. Repeat armhole decrease round every other round 4 times more, AT SAME TIME, after 6 (6, 6, 4) rounds have been worked from underarm bind-off round, ending with chart round 12 (14, 16, 20), shape V-neck as follows:

Neck decrease round (RS) Work steek stitches, k1, k2tog, work to last 3 stitches of round (working armhole decreases as established), SSK, k1. Repeat neck decrease round every 2nd (3rd, 3rd, 3rd) round 6 (11, 5, 7) times more, then every 3rd (0, 4th, 4th) round 5 (0, 6, 5) times—15 (17, 19, 21) stitches for each front shoulder, 51 (57, 63, 67) stitches for back. Bind off.

Sleeves

With A, cast on 34 (36, 38, 40) stitches, divided over 3 smaller double-pointed needles (dpns). Join and work in rounds as follows:

Begin rib pattern: Round 1 *K1, p1; repeat from*. Repeat last round 9 times more. Change to larger dpns. Begin with chart round 39 (41, 43, 1), work Stripe Pattern, AT SAME TIME, increase 1 stitch at each end of round every 6th round 10 times— 54 (56, 58, 60) stitches (change to circular needle when necessary). Work even until piece measures approximately 10" from beginning, ending with chart round 7 (9, 11, 17), and ending last round 4 stitches before end of round.

Shape cap

Next round Bind off 8 stitches (last 4 stitches of round and first 4 stitches of next round), work to end, pm, loop cast on 4 stitches (steek stitches), pm.

Decrease round K1, k2tog, knit to last 3 stitches, SSK, k1, work steek stitches. Continue in pattern and repeat decrease round every other round 4 (10, 14, 13) times more, then every round 11 (5, 3, 5) times—14 (16, 14, 14) stitches. Bind off.

Finishing

Block pieces. Secure steeks by working crochet chain stitch through every round of first and 4th stitch of steek. Cut through center of steeks. Sew shoulders. Set in sleeves.

Front and neck band

Place 5 markers along right front edge (for girl's), or left front edge (for boy's) for buttonholes, with the first ¾" above lower edge, the last at first V-neck decrease, and 3 others spaced evenly between. With RS facing, smaller 24" needle and A, begin at lower edge and pick up and knit 54 (56, 60, 62) stitches along right front edge to beginning of V-neck shaping, 22 (26, 32, 34) stitches to shoulder, 21 (23, 25, 25) stitches along back neck, 22 (26, 32, 34) stitches along left front V-neck, and 54 (56, 60, 62) stitches along left front edge—173 (187, 209, 217) stitches. Work 5 rows in k1, p1 rib, working buttonholes (yo, k2tog) at markers on 3rd row. Bind off. Whipstitch down crochet chain, while tucking ends under to neaten edges. Sew on buttons.

Size 6 SKACEL Sirenetta (cotton, acrylic; 50g; 121 yds) in 06 A and 05 B

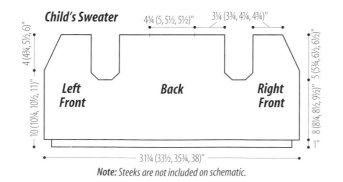

Child's Sweater

4¾ (5, 5½, 5½)"   3¼ (3¾, 4¼, 4¾)"

4 (4¾, 5½, 6)"

10 (10¼, 10½, 11)"

Left Front   **Back**   **Right Front**

5 (5¾, 6½, 6½)"

8 (8¼, 8½, 9½)"

1"

31¼ (33½, 35¾, 38)"

Note: *Steeks are not included on schematic.*

12 (12½, 13, 13½)"

3¼ (4, 4¾, 4¾)"

Sleeve

9"

1"

7½ (8, 8½, 9)"

> "Knitters often shy away from steeks because they seem dangerous and scary. Try a little teddy bear cardigan to practice this easy method. Then make a cardigan for your little one."
>
> —Rick Mondragon

Steek Tricks

Knitting in the round has many advantages. The right (public) side of the fabric is always visible to you; each line of the chart is read in the same direction; knitting seems faster since there is no need to stop and turn your work; and circular needles concentrate the weight of the work in your lap, reducing the stress on arms and wrists that is often associated with straight needles.

Circular knitting is ideal for making tubes—socks, hats, sleeves, and pullover bodies. (We'll deal with cardigans later.) Some sweater styles, such as yoke or raglan sweaters, can be made by joining the tubular sleeves and body, then shaping the shoulders all in one piece. However, a drop shoulder, modified drop, or set-in sleeve style causes knitting in the round to become a bit more challenging. One solution is to knit the upper portion of the sweater back and forth to accommodate armholes and necklines, but this is not necessarily the best way, for reasons of gauge and consistency. A better solution is the steek.

Steeks are commonly made by casting on a column of additional stitches that will be secured by machine stitching and then cut open to create armholes, necklines, or cardigan fronts. Many knitters shy away from steeks because they fear placing their handwork into a machine and then taking scissors to it. I have developed a way to avoid the sewing machine altogether, which is great for knitters who don't have access to one.

PLACING THE STEEKS IN A CARDIGAN

The bottom rib of a cardigan can be worked flat. Since it is usually composed of knits and purls in each row, knitting it flat is just as easy as working it in the round. Once you join the stitches and begin working the body in the round, add the steek for the cardigan opening between the first and last stitches of the row.

Adding the steek is easy. All you need to do is loop cast on stitches where you plan to have an opening. I suggest using 3–6 stitches in each steek. Whatever the stitch pattern of the body of the sweater, you must knit through the back loops of the first and last steek stitches every round. Twisting these stitches is the first step in securing the steek. (For colorwork like stranding and Fair Isle, I suggest you cast on 5 stitches and work them in alternating colors: MC, CC, MC, CC, MC.) When you reach the underarm you are ready to place the steeks for the armholes.

The type of armhole shaping depends on the style of the sweater. A drop-shoulder style has no armhole shaping. The steek stitches are added and the knitting continues uninterrupted. A modified drop (like Ted's sweater) involves one round with bind-offs at each underarm followed by a round to add the steek stitches. For a set-in style (like Sam's), bind off approximately half of the stitches to be decreased for each armhole in the first round, then add the steek and work a series of decrease rounds for the remaining shaping. These decreases are placed on both sides of the steek; usually, the decreases are separated from the steek by a knit stitch and are mirrored (paired) for full-fashioned decreases.

Steeks at the neck are treated similarly. For a V-neck, steek stitches are added at the base of the V, and paired decreases are worked on either side of the steek stitches at the usual intervals. Crew neck shaping begins approximately 3 inches from the final sweater length by binding off the base of the crew (usually about half the neck width), then casting on the steek stitches. Decreases are then made on either side of the steek stitches.

Sleeve steeks are worked according to the style of the armhole. A drop-style sleeve needs no steek. A modified drop requires a small steek which in length measures half the width of the armhole bind-off of the body underarm. An alternate method is to omit the steek and just work a few rows back and forth as in Ted's sweater. You can knit the sleeve cap of a set-in sleeve in the round using double-pointed needles and a steek. The underarm portion of a set-in sleeve is treated exactly the same as the underarm shaping of the body, with the same number of stitches bound off. The rest of the cap is then shaped with decreases on each side of the steek.

SECURING AND CUTTING THE STEEK

Once you have finished the knitting you are ready to secure the steek edges and cut the openings. Securing the steek stitches is typically done with two rows of machine stitching on both edges of the steek.

To secure the steek stitches without the machine, use a crochet hook. With knit side facing, fold the yarn on the wrong side of the garment and chain through the twisted edge stitch on each side of the steek (red yarn in photo). Working from bottom to top, work a chain stitch in every round. This secures the twist in each round, basically using the chain to form a knot in each stitch. You are now ready to cut down the center of the steek to form an opening.

If you are knitting an uneven number of steek stitches in alternating colors, it is easy to find and chain through the edge lines and then cut the center line of stitches. The contrasting-color strand is caught by the chain, which is sufficient to secure both yarns in the round.

SEAMING AND FINISHING

Sew in the sleeves, placing the seam one stitch into the body from the steek. Pick up stitches for a buttonband, armband, or neckband as you normally do.

NEATNESS

It is now time to sew in ends and neaten the openings. This step represents a small investment of time and effort, and the results are so rewarding.

The easiest method for neatening the cut edges is a whipstitch that tucks the ends under the crochet chain (yellow yarn in photo). It may

seem a little bulky at first, but blocking diminishes the bulk. You may also make a faced buttonband and tuck the cut ends into it. If your yarn is wool (not superwash), you may not need to do anything at this point. After the first few wearings and washings, just trim the edges if desired.

Steeks are a design tool and a real boon to circular knitting. Knowing that you can easily work shaping and openings into any garment frees you to knit to your desired silhouette in the round.

Lose your fear of cutting into your knitting by trying the little Teddy sweater. Then test the strength of the steek by tugging—the durability of the 'twist and chain' edge may well convince you to incorporate steeks into your next sweater.

6

In search of a novel idea for children who like options in their dressing, we offer a sweater worked in sections that get buttoned together, front and back. By creating versions of the same sweater, in different colors (we show brights and pastels), your child can pick which sections to button together every time it's worn.

Designed by Diane Zangl

Button Me

EASY +

LOOSE FIT

2 (4, 6, 8)
A 27 (28, 30, 32)"
B 11½ (13, 15½, 18)"

10cm/4"

30

22

• over stockinette stitch (knit on RS, purl on WS)

1 2 **3** 4 5 6

• Light weight
(Yarn amounts given are enough for 1 striped and 1 solid section)
A • 180 (210, 270, 335) yds
B • 220 (265, 330, 445) yds
C • 95 (115, 150, 180) yds
D • 120 (145, 190, 259) yds

• 4mm/US6
or size to obtain gauge

• 10 (10, 12, 12) 13mm/½"
various colors

&

• stitch markers

26

Notes
1 See *Techniques*, page 80, for SSK, lifted increase, and cable cast-on.
2 When working Narrow Stripe Pattern, carry yarns along side of work. **3** Follow color placement diagram for colors of each section.

Twisted rib (multiple of 4 sts, plus 2)
Row 1 (RS) [K1 through back loop (tbl)] twice, *p2, [k1 tbl] twice; repeat from*.
Row 2 [P1 tbl] twice, *k2, [p1 tbl] twice; repeat from*. Repeat Rows 1 and 2 for Twisted rib.

Wide Stripe Pattern
Work 10 rows each A, C, B, D; repeat from for Wide Stripe Pattern.

Narrow Stripe Pattern
Work 4 (0, 0, 0) rows A, then *work 4 rows each D, B, C, A; repeat from* for Narrow Stripe Pattern.

Section 1
Left Front or Right Back
Cast on 34 (34, 38, 42) stitches with

appropriate color. Work in Twisted rib for 1 (1, 1½, 1½)", increasing 0 (2, 1, 0) stitches on last WS row—34 (36, 39, 42) stitches. Work in stockinette stitch and appropriate pattern for 67 (79, 89, 109) rows. Piece measures approximately 10 (11½, 13½, 16)" from beginning.
Shape neck
Next row (WS) Bind off 7 (8, 8, 9) stitches, purl to end. Work 2 rows even.
Decrease row (RS) Knit to last 3 stitches, k2tog, k1. Repeat decrease row every other row 2 (2, 2, 3) times more—24 (25, 28, 29) stitches. Work 3 (3, 7, 5) rows even. Piece measures approximately 11½ (13, 15½, 18)" from beginning. Mark stitch at armhole edge for shoulder. Change to appropriate pattern.

Left Back or Right Front
Shape neck
Work 4 (4, 8, 6) rows even.
Increase row (RS) Knit to last 3 stitches, work right lifted increase, k2. Repeat increase row every other row 2 (2, 2, 3) times more. Work 2 rows even.
Next row (WS) Cable cast on 7 (8, 8,

Size 4 REYNOLDS Saucy Sport (cotton; 50g; 123 yds) Bright version in 360 (A), 143 (B), 63 (C), 44 (D); Pastel version in 370 (A), 150 (B), 553 (C), 869 (D)

Bright Version

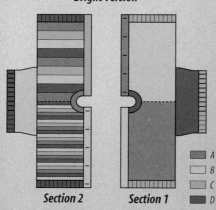

Section 2   Section 1

A
B
C
D

9) stitches, purl to end—34 (36, 39, 42) stitches. Work even until there are 78 (90, 104, 124) rows from shoulder marker and piece measures approximately 10½ (12, 14, 16½)", decrease 0 (2, 1, 0) stitches on last row—34 (34, 38, 42) stitches. Change color.

Next row (RS) [K1 tbl] twice, *k2, [k1 tbl] twice; repeat from*. Beginning with Row 2, work Twisted rib for 1 (1, 1½, 1½)". Bind off in pattern.

Section 2
Right Front or Left Back

Cast on with appropriate color and work rib as for Section 1—34 (36, 39, 42) stitches. Work in stockinette stitch and appropriate pattern for 68 (80, 90, 110) rows.

Shape neck

Next row (RS) Bind off 7 (8, 8, 9) stitches, knit to end. Work 1 row even.

Decrease row (RS) K1, SSK, knit to end. Repeat decrease row every other row 2 (2, 2, 3) times more—24 (25, 28, 29) stitches. Work 3 (3, 7, 5) rows even. Piece measures approximately 11½ (13, 15½, 18)" from beginning. Mark stitch at armhole edge for shoulder. Change pattern.

Right Back or Left Front

Shape neck

Work 4 (4, 8, 6) rows even.

Increase row (RS) K2, work left lifted increase, knit to end. Repeat increase

row every other row 2 (2, 2, 3) times more. Work 1 row even.

Next row (RS) Cable cast on 7 (8, 8, 9) stitches, knit to end—34 (36, 39, 42) stitches. Complete as for Section 1.

First Sleeve

Cast on 46 (50, 54, 62) stitches with appropriate color. Work in Twisted rib for ¾ (¾, 1, 1)", end with a WS row. Change to appropriate color. Work in stockinette stitch, increasing 1 stitch each side on 5th (5th, 5th, 11th) row, then every 8th (6th, 6th, 10th) row 1 (2, 2, 1) times—50 (56, 60, 66) stitches. Work even until piece measures 3 (3½, 4, 4½)" from beginning. Bind off.

Second Sleeve

Work as for first sleeve, with appropriate colors.

Finishing

Neckbands

With RS facing and appropriate color, pick up and knit 34 (38, 42, 46) stitches along neck edge. Beginning with Row 2, work in Twisted rib for ¾ (¾, 1, 1)". Bind off in pattern.

Buttonbands

With RS facing and appropriate color, begin at neck edge and pick up and knit 58 (66, 78, 94) stitches along center edge. Beginning with Row 2, work in Twisted rib for 1". Bind off in pattern.

Buttonhole bands

(**Note** Bind off 2 stitches for each buttonhole; on following row, cast on 2 stitches over each pair of bound-off stitches.)

Place 5 (5, 6, 6) markers for buttonholes along center edge, with the first and last ½" from neck and lower edges, and 3 (3, 4, 4) others spaced evenly between. With RS facing and appropriate color, begin at lower edge and pick up and knit 58 (66, 78, 94) stitches along center edge. Work as for buttonband, working buttonholes at markers when band measures ½". Place marker 4½ (5, 5½, 6)" on each side of each shoulder marker for armholes. Sew sleeves between armhole markers. Sew side and sleeve seams. Sew on buttons.

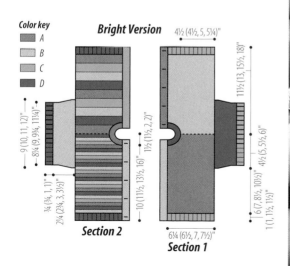

Color key
- A
- B
- C
- D

Bright Version

Section 2

Section 1

Visit knittinguniverse.com to design your own color scheme with Knitter's Paintbox.

Gray flannel jumpers and plaid skirts are so adorable on young girls. When the skirt is unbottoned, buttonholes in the tunic's double-knit hem can be trimmed with cuff-link buttons, bows, or a drawstring.

Designed by Knitter's Design Team

Schoolgirl Charmer

INTERMEDIATE +

B A

LOOSE FIT

2 (4, 8, 12)
A 25 (28½, 32, 35½)"
B JUMPER 23¾ (25¼, 28½, 31)"
B TUNIC ONLY 16½ (17½, 18½, 19)"

10cm/4"

29

23

• over stockinette stitch (knit on RS, purl on WS) using larger needles

1 2 **3** 4 5 6

• Light weight
A • 500 (600, 800, 900) yds
B • 300 (300, 400, 450) yds
C • 150 yds

• 2.75mm/US2 and 3.75mm/US5, or size to obtain gauge

• 3.75mm/US5, 40cm/16" long

&
• stitch marker

• 14 (16, 18, 20) 15mm/⅝"

30

Note

See *Techniques,* page 80, for SSK, duplicate stitch, and tubular cast-on.

TUNIC
Back

Work double-knit hem

With smaller needles and A, cast on 140 (160, 180, 200) stitches, using tubular cast-on. Change to larger needles.
Begin double-knit fabric: Row 1 *K1, slip 1 purlwise with yarn in front; repeat from*. Repeat last row 15 times more (8 rows each side).
Buttonhole Row 1 Work 8 stitches, *SSK, yo, work 18 stitches; repeat from* 5 (6, 7, 8) times more, end SSK, yo, work last 10 stitches.
Next row Work Double-knit fabric, knitting yo and slipping SSK.
Work even in Double-knit fabric for 16 rows more (8 rows each side).
Work single-layer body
Next row (RS) *SSK; repeat from* across—70 (80, 90, 100) stitches.

Next row Purl, increasing 2 stitches evenly—72 (82, 92, 102) stitches. Work even in stockinette stitch until piece measures 10½ (11½, 12, 12½)" from beginning, end with a WS row.
Shape armholes
Bind off 6 (6, 8, 8) stitches at beginning of next 2 rows. Decrease 1 stitch each side every RS row 4 (5, 5, 6) times—52 (60, 66, 74) stitches. Work even until armhole measures 6 (6, 6½, 6½)". Bind off.

Front

Work as for back until armhole measures 3", end with a WS row.
Shape neck
Next row (RS) K18 (22, 24, 27), join 2nd ball of yarn and bind off center 16 (16, 18, 20) stitches, knit to end. Working both sides at same time, decrease 1 stitch at each neck edge every RS row 7 times—11 (15, 17, 20) stitches each side. Work even until armhole measures same length as back to shoulder. Bind off.

Size 4 PLYMOUTH Encore DK (wool, acrylic; 50g; 150 yds) in 389 (A), 9601 (B), 848 (C)

Finishing

Block pieces. Sew shoulder and side seams.

Neck edging

With RS facing and circular needle, begin at right shoulder and pick up and knit 30 (30, 32, 34) stitches evenly along back neck, 21 (21, 24, 24) stitches along left front neck, 16 (16, 18, 20) stitches along center front neck, and 21 (21, 24, 24) stitches along right front neck—88 (88, 98, 102) stitches. Place marker, join and knit 8 rounds. Bind off loosely. Fold edging to inside and baste down.

Armhole edging

Work as for neck edging, picking up 82 (82, 92, 92) stitches evenly around armhole edge.

SKIRT
Back

With A, cast on 72 (82, 92, 102) stitches.
Begin Seed Stitch: Row 1 (RS) * K1, p1; repeat from *.
Row 2 * P1, k1; repeat from *.
Repeat Rows 1 and 2 twice more. Work 4 rows in stockinette stitch. Work Rows 1–24 of Chart for Skirt—87 (99, 111, 123) stitches. Work 16-row repeat 2 (2, 3, 4) times. Cut A and C. Continue with B only.

Work hem

Next row (RS) Knit.
Knit next row on WS for turning ridge.
[Knit 1 row, purl 1 row] 3 times. Bind off.

Front

Work as for back.

Finishing

Work vertical columns of duplicate stitch over slipped stitches of Chart pattern, alternating A and C.
Sew side seams. Sew buttons on band at the transition from Seed stitch to stockinette stitch, centered over C stripes. Fold hem to WS at turning ridge and sew in place.

Give your tunic added personality with 'cuff-link' buttons (two buttons sewn back to back). Each button can offer a different look—perfect for dressing up or down. The tunic's double-knit hem with buttonholes on both layers makes this versatility possible.

Chart for Skirt

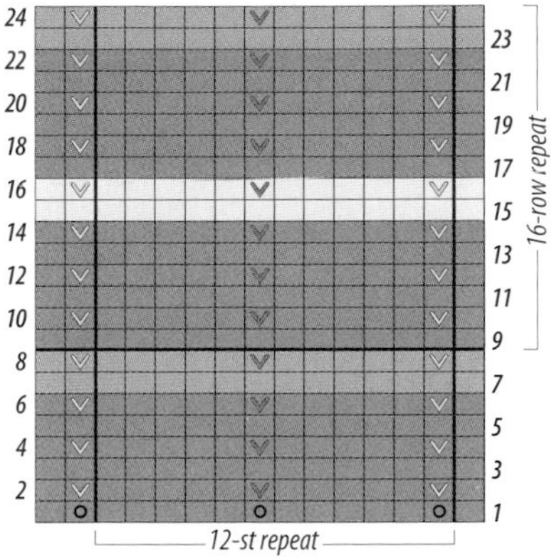
24
22
20
18
16
14
12
10
8
6
4
2
23
21
19
17
15
13
11
9
7
5
3
1
16-row repeat
12-st repeat

Color key

- A
- B
- C

Stitch key

- K on RS, p on WS
- Yo
- Sl 1 purlwise with yarn in front
- after skirt is knit, work in duplicate st with A
- after skirt is knit, work in duplicate st with C

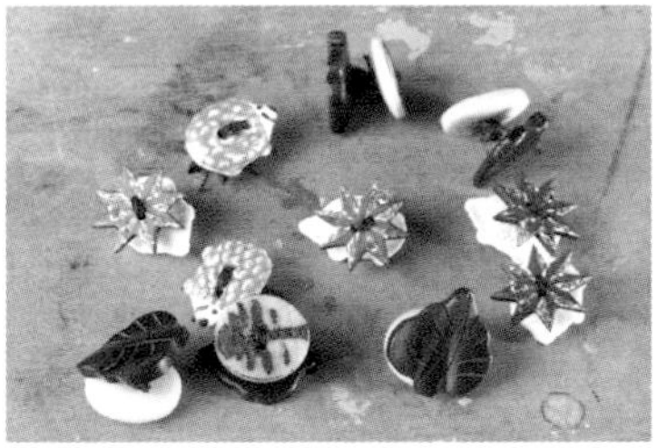

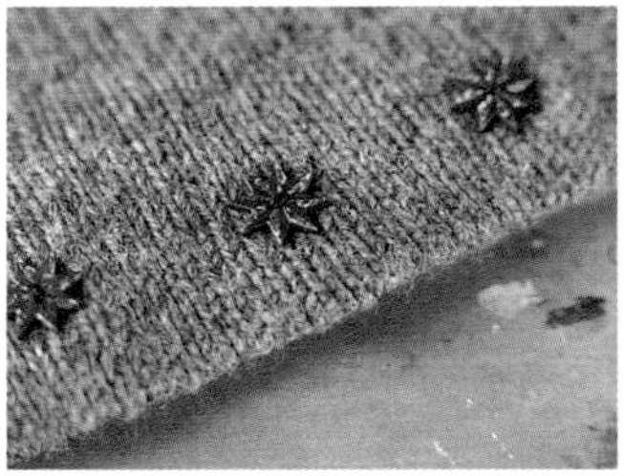

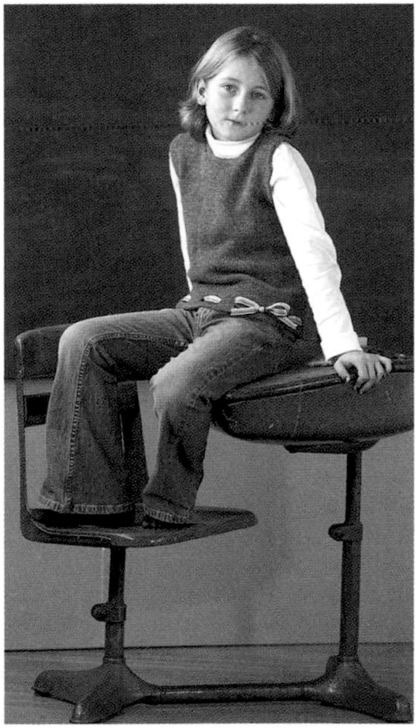

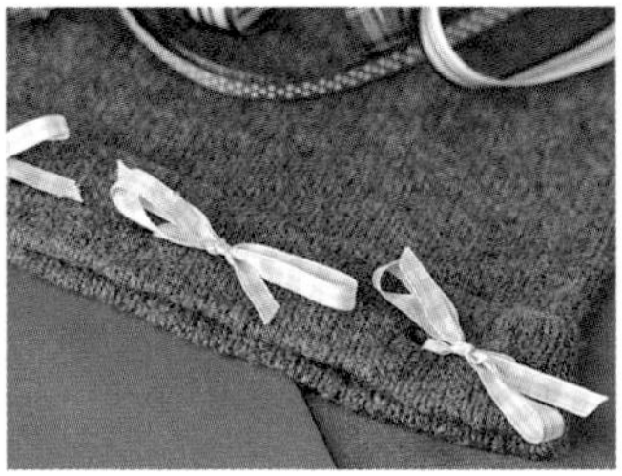

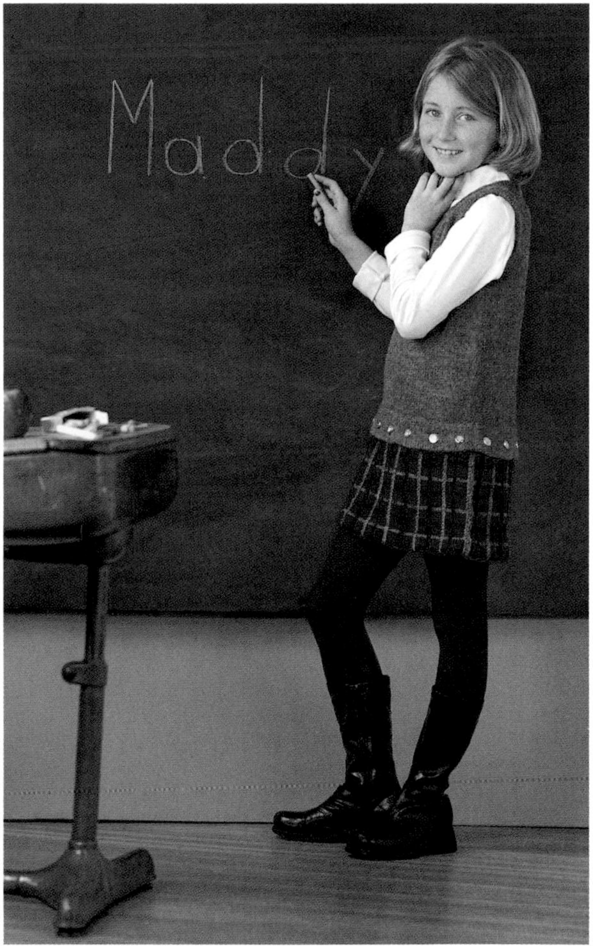
Maddy

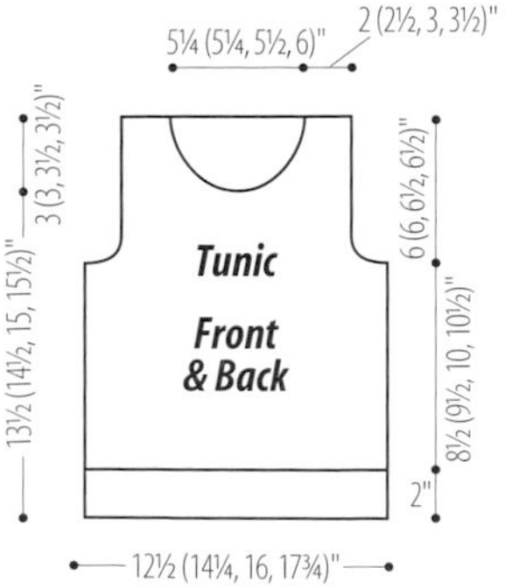
5¼ (5¼, 5½, 6)"
2 (2½, 3, 3½)"
3 (3, 3½, 3½)"
13½ (14½, 15, 15½)"
6 (6, 6½, 6½)"
8½ (9½, 10, 10½)"
2"
Tunic
Front
& Back
12½ (14¼, 16, 17¾)"

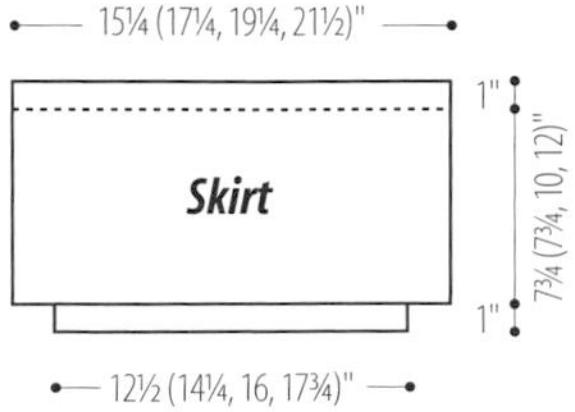
15¼ (17¼, 19¼, 21½)"
1"
7¾ (7¾, 10, 12)"
1"
Skirt
12½ (14¼, 16, 17¾)"

African violets are tropical plants from the gloxinia family, widely grown as a houseplant. Here is a chance to pay them reverence in the regal colors of their namesake—violets.

Designed by Rick Mondragon

African Violets

INTERMEDIATE

STANDARD FIT

2 (4, 6)
A 25¼ (27½, 29¾)"
B 15½ (16¼, 17¼)"

10cm/4"

24

18

• over stockinette stitch (knit on RS, purl on WS), using larger needles

1 2 3 **4** 5 6

Medium weight
A–F • 95 yds each color

• 5mm/US8, or size to obtain gauge, 60cm/24" long
• 4mm/US6, 40cm/16" and 60cm/24" long

• 5mm/H-8 for cast-on
• 1.25mm/8 steel for placing beads

&

• stitch holders and marker
• approximately 70 (75, 80) 5mm or E beads in yellow

34

Notes

1 See *Techniques*, page 80, for picking up stitches in a chain and 3-needle bind-off. **2** Vest is worked in one piece to underarm, then divided for fronts and back. **3** Slip stitches purlwise with yarn at WS of work.

Body

With larger crochet hook and waste yarn, chain 107 (117, 127), plus a few extra. Break yarn. ***Begin Chart Pattern: Row 5 (3, 1)*** (RS) With loop end of chain at the left, use larger needle and B to pick up and knit 87 (89, 95) stitches in center of chain, leaving at least 10 (14, 16) chains at each side.
Row 6 (4, 2) (WS) Work chart pattern to end, then pick up and purl 3 stitches in chain.
Row 7 (5, 3) Work chart pattern to end, then pick up and knit 3 stitches in chain. Continue following chart for pattern and picked-up stitches through chart row 15 (19, 17)—107 (117, 127) stitches. Continue in chart pattern through row 47. Piece measures approximately 7¼ (7½, 7¾)" from beginning.

Divide for fronts and back
Next row (WS) P24 (26, 29) and place remaining stitches on hold.

Left Front
Shape armhole
Decrease 1 stitch at beginning of every RS row 3 times—21 (23, 26) stitches. Work even through chart row 60. Armhole measures approximately 2¼".
Shape neck
Decrease 1 stitch at end of next RS row, then every other row 10 times more, then every 4th row 0 (0, 2) times, every 10th row 0 (1, 0) time—10 (11, 13) stitches. Work even through chart row 91 (95, 99). Armhole measures approximately 7½ (8, 8¾)". Place stitches on hold.

Right Front
Place 24 (26, 29) stitches on needle, ready to work a WS row, leaving center 59 (65, 69) stitches on hold. Work to correspond to left front, reversing shaping. Work armhole decreases at end of RS rows and neck decreases at beginning of RS rows.

Size 6 BROWN SHEEP Lamb's Pride (wool, mohair; 114g; 190 yds) in M59 (A), M65 (B) and M62 (C); Top of the Lamb (wool; 114g; 190 yds) in 461 (D), 462 (E) and 456 (F)

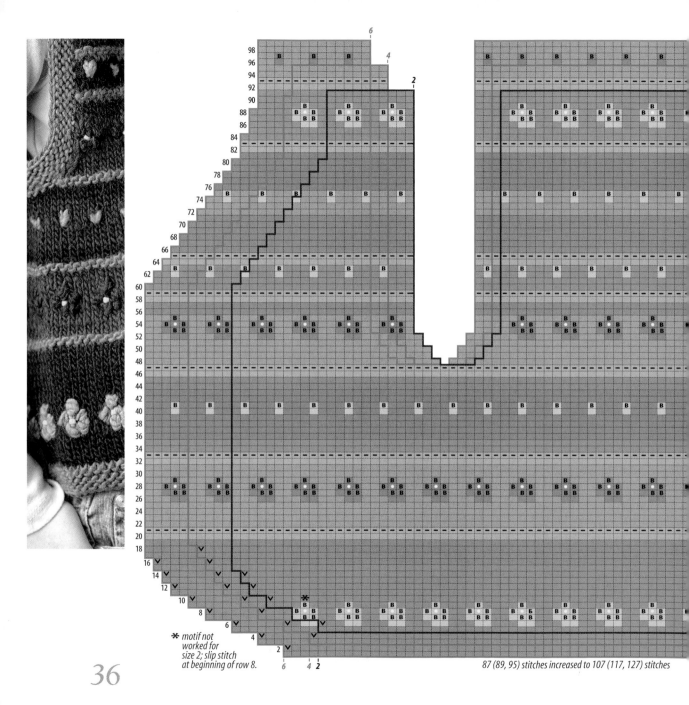

*motif not
worked for
size 2; slip stitch
at beginning of row 8.

36

87 (89, 95) stitches increased to 107 (117, 127) stitches

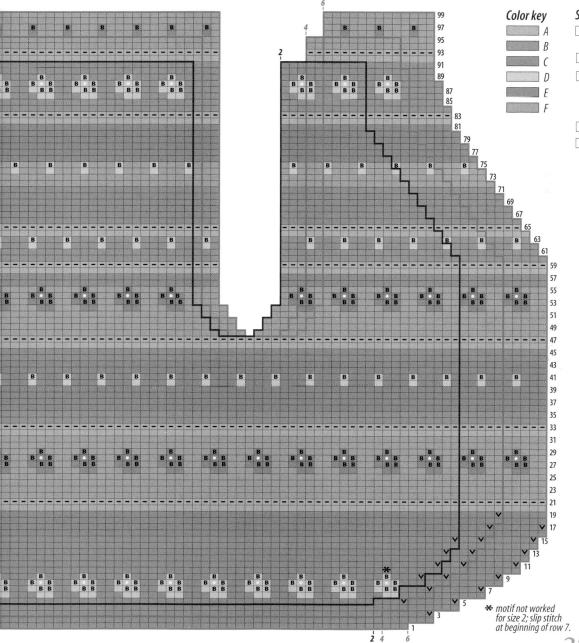

Color key

- A
- B
- C
- D
- E
- F

Stitch key

- ☐ Knit on RS, purl on WS
- − Purl on RS
- ☑ Slip 1 purlwise with yarn at WS of work
- **B** Make Bobble
- ☐ Place Bead

✳ motif not worked for size 2; slip stitch at beginning of row 7.

37

Back

Place center 51 (53, 57) stitches on needle, ready to work a WS row, leaving 4 (6, 6) stitches at each side on hold for underarms.

Shape armholes

Decrease 1 stitch each side every RS row 3 times—45 (47, 51) stitches. Work even through chart row 91 (95, 99). Place stitches on hold.

Finishing

With B (F, F) join shoulders, using 3-needle bind-off, as follows: join 10 (11, 13) stitches of first shoulder, bind off back neck stitches until 10 (11, 13) stitches remain, join 2nd shoulder.

Armhole bands

With RS facing, 16" needle, and A, beginning at center of underarm, knit 2 (3, 3) stitches from holder, pick up and knit 32 (35, 38) stitches to shoulder, 1 stitch in shoulder seam, then 32 (35, 38) stitches along other half of armhole, knit 2 (3, 3) stitches from holder—69 (77, 83) stitches. Place marker, join, and [purl 1 round, knit 1 round] twice, purl 1 round. Bind off knitwise.

Neck, fronts, and lower edge band

With RS facing, larger 24" needle and A, pick up and knit 25 stitches along back neck, 57 (57, 61) stitches along left front edge, then knit 107 (117, 127) stitches from chain, removing waste yarn as you go, pick up and knit 57 (57, 61) stitches along right front edge—246 (256, 274) stitches. Work as for armhole bands, decreasing 10 stitches evenly across straight portion of lower edge on first row. Bind off. Block vest.

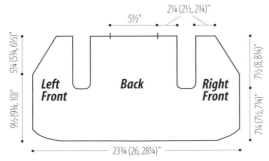

5½"

2¼ (2½, 2¾)"

5¼ (5¾, 6½)"

Left Front

Back

Right Front

7½ (8, 8¾)"

9½ (9¾, 10)"

7¼ (7½, 7¾)"

23¾ (26, 28¼)"

A NEW BOBBLE

These bobbles are made both on right-side (knit) and wrong-side (purl) rows with a k1-yo-k1 or p1-yo-p1 increase done around a stitch rather than into a stitch (1). The increases and the wrapped stitch are then immediately bound off with the background color.

RS BOBBLE

1 Insert right needle between stitches as shown, then with CC, k1, yo, k1.

2 Slip the 3 stitches to left needle.

3 Lay background strand over left needle from back to front. With right needle, pull 4 stitches over strand, one at a time. With yarn in back, slip stitch to right needle.

WS BOBBLE

1 Insert right needle between stitches as shown, then with CC, p1, yo, p1.

2 Slip the 3 stitches to left needle.

3 Work as for Step 3 of RS Bobble, but slip stitch to right needle with yarn in front.

DRAWING-ON A BEAD

1 Purl the stitch you want to carry the bead. Insert crochet hook through the bead.

2 With the hook, pull the stitch off the needle and through the bead.

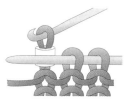

3 Place the stitch on the needle, being careful not to twist it.

4 Tighten the yarn and continue.

39

9

INTERMEDIATE

OVERSIZED FIT

4 (6, 8, 10)
A 30 (31½, 33½, 35)"
B 15 (15¾, 17½, 18¼)"
C 18 (20, 20½, 22½)"

10cm/4"

26

18

• over stockinette stitch (knit on RS, purl on WS) using larger needles

1 2 3 **4** 5 6

• Medium weight
MC • 525 (615, 705, 795) yds
A • 350 (410, 470, 530) yds
B • 60 (60, 65, 65) yds
C • 35 (35, 40, 40) yds
D • 30 (30, 30, 30) yds

• 4mm/US6 and 4.5mm/US7, or size to obtain gauge

• 4mm/US6, 40cm/16" long

Here's a true blue-collar knit for your crew.

Road Work

Note
See *Techniques*, page 80, for intarsia and duplicate stitch.

Stripe Pattern
Work in stockinette stitch as follows:
6 rows MC, 4 rows A; repeat from for Stripe Pattern.

Back
*With smaller needles and MC, cast on 66 (70, 74, 78) stitches. Work 13 rows of Chart A (see page 42), increasing 1 stitch on last (WS) row—67 (71, 75, 79) stitches. Change to larger needles.
Begin Chart B: Row 1 (RS) Beginning as indicated for back (for the size you are making), work first 0 (2, 4, 6) stitches of chart, then work 6-stitch repeat 5 times, work 7 center stitches of chart, then work next 6-stitch repeat 5 times, work last 0 (2, 4, 6) stitches of chart, ending as indicated. Continue in pattern through chart row 7.*
Work in Stripe Pattern for 0 (10, 20, 20) rows.
Begin Chart C: Row 1 (WS) With MC, p18 (20, 22, 24), place marker (pm), work 31 stitches of Chart C, pm, purl to end.

Continue working Chart C between markers and Stripe Pattern over stitches at each side, through chart row 66, then continue Stripe Pattern on all stitches for 7 (3, 3, 9) rows more. Piece measures approximately 14½ (15¼, 17, 17¾)" from beginning.
Shape neck
Next row (RS) Work 22 (23, 23, 25) stitches, join 2nd ball of yarn and bind off center 23 (25, 29, 29) stitches, work to end. Working both sides at same time, work 1 row even. Decrease 1 stitch each side of neck on next row. Work 1 row even. Bind off remaining 21 (22, 22, 24) stitches each side for shoulders.

Front
Work from *to* of back, then work in Stripe Pattern for 10 (10, 20, 20) rows.
Begin Chart D: Row 1 (WS) With MC, p9 (11, 13, 15), pm, work 49 stitches of Chart D, pm, purl to end. Continue working Chart D between markers and Stripe Pattern over stitches at each side, through chart row 46, then continue Stripe Pattern on all stitches for 7 (13, 13, 19) rows more. Piece measures approximately 12¾ (13½, 15¼, 16)" from beginning.

• stitch markers

• two 22mm/⅞"

Chart C

65 64 63 62 61 60 59 58 57 56 55 54 53 52 51 50 49 48 47 46 45 44 43 42 41 40 39 38 37 36 35 34 33 32 31 30 29 28 27 26 25 24 23 22 21 20 19 18 17 16 15 14 13 12 11 10 9 8 7 6 5 4 3 2 1

31 sts

Color Key

- MC
- A
- B
- C
- D

(Duplicate st with D on Chart C)

Stitch Key

- ☐ K on RS, p on WS
- ▬ P on RS, k on WS
- ╲ Chain st with D

Size 8 BERNAT Berella 4 (acrylic; 100g; 240 yds) in 8860 (MC); 8846 (A); 8933 (B); 8886 (C), and 8994 (D)

Chart B

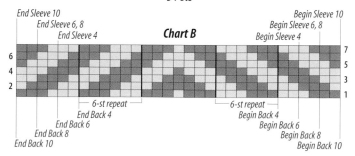

End Sleeve 10
End Sleeve 6, 8
End Sleeve 4

Begin Sleeve 10
Begin Sleeve 6, 8
Begin Sleeve 4

7 6 5 4 3 2 1

6-st repeat
End Back 4

6-st repeat
Begin Back 4

End Back 6
End Back 8
End Back 10

Begin Back 6
Begin Back 8
Begin Back 10

41

Chart D

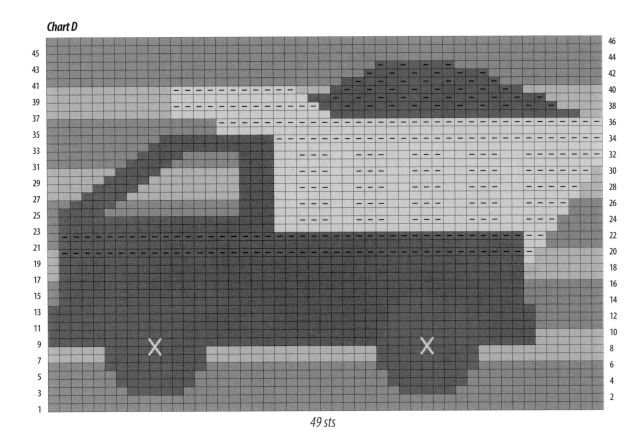

49 sts

Chart A

4-st repeat

Color Key
- MC
- A
- B
- C
- D
(Duplicate st with D on Chart C)

Stitch Key
- K on RS, p on WS
- — P on RS, k on WS

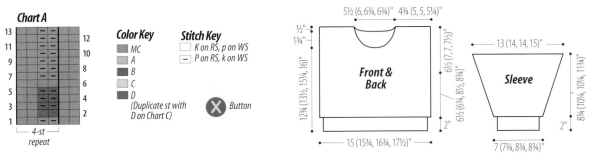

Button

Front & Back

5½ (6, 6¾, 6¾)" 4¾ (5, 5, 5¼)"

½"
1¾"

6½ (7, 7, 7½)"

12¾ (13½, 15¼, 16)"

6½ (6¾, 8½, 8¾)"

2"

15 (15¾, 16¾, 17½)"

Sleeve

13 (14, 14, 15)"

8¾ (10¼, 10¼, 11¾)"

2"

7 (7¾, 8¾, 8¾)"

Shape neck
Next row (RS) Work 29 (30, 31, 33) stitches, join 2nd ball of yarn and bind off center 9 (11, 13, 13) stitches, work to end. Working both sides at same time, bind off from each neck edge 3 stitches 0 (0, 1, 1) time, 2 stitches 2 (2, 1, 1) times, then decrease 1 stitch each side of neck every RS row 4 times—21 (22, 22, 24) stitches each side. Work 1 row even. Bind off.

Sleeves

With smaller needles and MC, cast on 30 (34, 38, 38) stitches. Work 13 rows of Chart A, increasing 1 stitch on last (WS) row—31 (35, 39, 39) stitches. Change to larger needles. Work in stockinette stitch and Stripe Pattern as follows: [4 rows A, 6 rows MC] 5 (6, 6, 7) times, AT SAME TIME, increase 1 stitch each side (working increases into Stripe Pattern) on 3rd (5th, 5th, 5th) row, then every 2nd (4th, 4th, 4th) row 3 (12, 6, 7) times, every 4th (6th, 6th, 6th) row 10 (1, 5, 6) times—59 (63, 63, 67) stitches. When last row of Stripe Pattern has been worked, work 7 rows of Chart B, beginning and ending as indicated for sleeve, and working each 6-stitch repeat 4 times. Bind off.

Finishing
Sew shoulders.
Neckband
With RS facing, circular needle and MC, begin at left shoulder and pick up and knit 68 (72, 76, 76) stitches evenly around neck edge. Pm, join and work 4-stitch repeat of Chart A for 13 rounds (working each chart row on RS). Bind off in pattern. Sew 2 buttons on wheels of Chart D motif on front. Work chain stitch and duplicate stitch on Chart C motif on back. Place markers 6½ (7, 7, 7½)" down from shoulders on front and back for armholes. Sew sleeves between markers. Sew side and sleeve seams.

Here's a design for a kid's jacket that's warm, brightly colored, and easy to make. It's a design that looks great in a variety of color combinations or in one variegated yarn..

Designed by Celeste Pinheiro

Garter Stitch Jacket

it's easy
...go for it!

EASY +

OVERSIZED FIT

2 (4/6, 8/10)
A 28 (32, 35½)"
B 13½ (15½, 17½)"
C 18 (20, 22)"

10cm/4"

28 | 14

• over garter stitch (knit every row)

1 2 3 4 **5** 6

• Bulky weight
MC • 295 (390, 495) yds
A • 225 (255, 300) yds
B • 85 (110, 140) yds
C • 45 (45, 45) yds
or
645 (780, 975) yds
for one-color version

• 6mm/US10, or size to obtain gauge,
60cm/24" long

• four 25mm/1"

• stitch holders

Notes
1 See *Techniques*, page 80, for tassels.
2 Jacket is worked back and forth in one piece to underarm, then divided and fronts and back are worked separately.
3 For ease of working, mark RS of piece.
4 Instructions are for multicolored version on page 47.

Pockets (make 2)
With C, cast on 17 stitches. Work in garter stitch for 5". Bind off.

Body
With MC, cast on 91 (105, 117) stitches. Work in garter stitch for 7 (8½, 10)", end with a WS row.
Divide for underarms: Next row (RS) Knit 21 (24, 27) stitches and place these stitches on a holder for right front, knit 49 (57, 63) stitches and place these stitches on a holder for back, knit 21 (24, 27) stitches for left front and continue on these stitches.

Left Front
Work even until armhole measures 4¾ (5¼, 5¾)", end with a RS row.

Shape neck: Next row (WS) Bind off 4 stitches, knit to end.
Next row Knit to last 2 stitches, k2tog. Continue to decrease 1 stitch at neck edge every other row 4 times more—12 (15, 18) stitches. Work even until armhole measures 6½ (7, 7½)". Bind off.

Back
With WS facing, join yarn at underarm and work even until back measures same length as left front to shoulder. Bind off.

Right Front
Work as for left front, reversing neck shaping by working bind-off and decreases at beginning of RS rows.

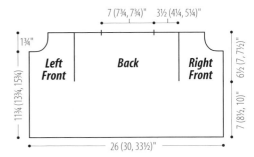

7 (7¾, 7¾)"   3½ (4¼, 5¼)"

1¾"

11¾ (13¾, 15¾)"

Left Front   **Back**   **Right Front**

6½ (7, 7½)"

7 (8½, 10)"

26 (30, 33½)"

Size 4/6 NORO Iro (wool, silk; 100g; 132 yds) in 54

Sleeves

With A, cast on 25 (25, 27) stitches. Work in garter stitch, increasing 1 stitch each side every 6th row 5 (9, 10) times, then every 8th row 5 (3, 3) times—45 (49, 53) stitches. Work even until piece measures 11 (12, 13)" from beginning. Bind off.

Hood

With B, cast on 53 (61, 69) stitches. Work in garter stitch for 3½ (4, 4)", end with a WS row. Increase 1 stitch each side on next row, then every other row 4 times more—63 (71, 79) stitches. Work even until piece measures 6 (7, 7)" from beginning. Place stitches on hold.

Finishing

Block pieces. Sew shoulder seams. Fold hood in half and sew side edges around neck edge, with cast-on edge falling at center back neck. Sew hood seam.

Front and hood band

With RS facing and A, begin at lower edge and pick up and knit 41 (48, 55) stitches evenly along right front edge, knit 63 (71, 79) stitches of hood on hold, then pick up and knit 41 (48, 55) stitches along left front edge—145 (167, 189) stitches.

Work in garter stitch for 11 rows, making buttonholes on row 6 as follows: knit 7 (8, 11) stitches, *bind off 3 stitches, knit 5 (7, 8) more stitches; repeat from* twice more, bind off 3 stitches, knit to end. On next row, cast on 3 stitches over each set of bound-off stitches. Bind off. Sew pockets on fronts, ¾" in from front band and 1½ (2, 3)" above lower edge. Make optional tassel from strands of all 4 colors and sew to point of hood. Sew buttons on left front band, opposite buttonholes.

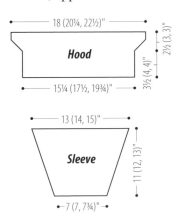

Page 47 Size 4/6 BERNAT Quick and Easy (acrylic; 85g; 130 yds) 6664 (MC); 6216 (A); 6618 (B) and 6328 (C)

Visit knittinguniverse.com to design your own color scheme with Knitter's Paintbox.

Mittens and gloves are important accessories in cold weather, but especially easy for children to misplace. Kathy's idea of adding mitten and glove pockets to these classic cardigans is clever and unbelievably practical.

Designed by Kathy Cheifetz

Pockets for Two

INTERMEDIATE +

2 (4, 6, 8)
A 28 (30, 32, 34)"
B 16¼ (17, 18, 19¼)"
C 18 (19½, 21, 22½)"

10cm/4"

20

16

• over stockinette stitch (knit on RS, purl on WS) using 6mm/US10 needles and 2 strands of yarn

1 2 **3** 4 5 6

• Light weight
Both versions
MC • 840 (950, 1060, 1250) yds
Glove Pocket version
A–E • 45 yds of each
F • 150 yds
Mitten Pocket version
A • 275 (315, 350, 410) yds
B • 160 (180, 200, 230) yds

• 2.75mm/US2, 3.25mm/US3, 5mm/US8, and 6mm/US10 needles
or size to obtain gauge

Notes

1 See *Techniques*, page 80, for SSK, Make 1 (M1), loop cast-on, 3-needle bind-off, and pompons. *2* Sweaters are worked with 2 strands of yarn held together, except for the pockets, which are worked with single strands.

GIRL'S GLOVE VERSION

Back

With 6mm/US10 needles and 2 strands of MC, cast on 53 (57, 61, 65) stitches.
Begin rib: Row 1 (RS) *K1, p1; repeat from*, end k1. Work 5 more rows in rib, increasing 3 stitches evenly across last row—56 (60, 64, 68) stitches. Work in stockinette stitch until piece measures 11 (11, 12, 12)" from beginning, end with a WS row.

Shape armholes

Bind off 5 stitches at beginning of next 2 rows—46 (50, 54, 58) stitches. Work

3mm/D

• six 15mm/⅝" (glove pocket version)
• six 20mm/¾" (mitten pocket version)

&

• stitch holders and markers

even until armhole measures 4½ (5¼, 5¼, 6½)", end with a WS row.
Shape neck
Next row (RS) K14 (15, 16, 18), join 2nd ball of yarn and bind off center 18 (20, 22, 22) stitches, knit to end. Working both sides at same time, decrease 1 st at each neck edge on next RS row. Work 1 row even. Place remaining 13 (14, 15, 17) stitches each side on hold.

Right Front

With 6mm/US10 needles and 2 strands of MC, cast on 31 (33, 35, 37) stitches. Work 2 rows in k1, p1 rib.
Buttonhole row (RS) K1, p1, k1, bind off 1 stitch, rib to end.
Next row Rib to last 3 stitches, loop cast on 1 stitch over bound-off stitch, p1, k1, p1. Rib 1 row.
Next row (WS) Rib to last 7 stitches, increasing 2 sts evenly across, place remaining 7 stitches on hold for front band—26 (28, 30, 32) stitches. Work in stockinette stitch until piece measures same length as back to underarm, end with a RS row.

Shape armhole

Next row (WS) Bind off 5 stitches, purl to end—21 (23, 25, 27) stitches. Work even until armhole measures 3¼ (4, 3½, 4¾)", end with a WS row.

Shape neck

Next row (RS) Bind off 3 stitches (neck edge), knit to end. Decrease 1 stitch at neck edge every row 5 (6, 7, 7) times—13 (14, 15, 17) stitches. Work even until armhole measures same length as back to shoulder. Place stitches on hold.

Left Front

With 6mm/US10 needles and 2 strands of MC held together, cast on 31 (33, 35, 37) stitches. Work 6 rows in k1, p1 rib as for back, working last (WS) row as follows: Rib 7 stitches and place these stitches on hold for front band, rib to end, increasing 2 stitches evenly across—26 (28, 30, 32) stitches. Complete to correspond to right front, reversing shaping.

Sleeves

With 5mm/US8 needles and 2 strands of MC held together, cast on 21 (23, 23, 25) stitches. Work in k1, p1 rib for 2½", increasing 7 (9, 9, 11) stitches evenly across last (WS) row—28 (32, 32, 36) stitches. Change to 6mm/US10 needles. Work in stockinette stitch and Stripe Pattern as follows: Work 2 rows each with *MC, A, MC, B, MC, C, MC, D, MC, E, MC, F; repeat from* (24 rows), AT SAME TIME, increase 1 stitch each side on 7th (5th, 7th, 5th) row, then every 6th (6th, 6th, 4th) row 6 (7, 5, 4) times,

Size 6 PATONS *Look At Me (acrylic, nylon; 50g; 152 yds) Glove Pocket Version in 6364 (MC), 6385 (A), 6370 (B), 6365 (C), 6366 (D), 6367 (E), and 6368 (F)*

49

every 0 (0, 8th, 6th) row 0 (0, 2, 6) times—42 (48, 48, 58) stitches. Piece measures approximately 11 (12, 13, 14)" from beginning. Place marker each side of row for underarm. Work 1¼" even. Bind off.

Right Glove Pocket
(**Note** Work gloves with single strand of yarn.)
Work cuff
With 3.25mm/US3 needles and E, cast on 23 stitches. Work in k1, p1 rib in Stripe Pattern as follows: 1 row E, then 2 rows each D, C, and B, 4 rows A, then 2 rows each B, C, D and E. Bind off with E.
Shape palm and base of thumb
With RS of cuff facing, 3.25mm/US3 needles and F, pick up and knit 23 stitches along cast-on edge.
Row 1 (WS) Purl.
Row 2 Knit to last st, M1, k1.
Rows 3–10 Repeat Rows 1 and 2 four times—28 stitches. Work 6 rows even.
Next row (WS) Bind off 3 stitches, purl to end—25 stitches.
Next row Knit to last 2 stitches, SSK—24 stitches (thumb base complete). Work 8 rows even. Piece measures approximately 2¾" above cuff.
Shape fingers
Little Finger
Next row (WS) P18 and place these stitches on hold. With A, work last 6 stitches as follows: P1,

loop cast on 1 stitch, p4, loop cast on 1 stitch, p1—8 stitches. Work 9 rows even.
Shape top
Next row (WS) [P2tog] 4 times—4 stitches.
Next row [K2tog] twice—2 stitches.
Next row P2tog. Fasten off last stitch.

Index Finger
Place 18 stitches from holder onto needle, ready to work a RS row.
Next row (RS) With F, k12 and place these stitches on hold. With D, work last 6 stitches as follows: K1, loop cast on 1 stitch, k4, loop cast on 1 stitch, k1—8 stitches. Work 11 rows even.
Shape top
Next row (RS) [K2tog] 4 times—4 stitches.
Next row [P2tog] twice—2 stitches.
Next row K2tog. Fasten off last stitch.

Ring Finger
Place 12 stitches from holder onto needle, ready to work a WS row.
Next row (WS) With F, p6 and place these stitches on hold. With B, work last 6 stitches as follows: P1, loop cast on 1 stitch, p4, loop cast on 1 stitch, p1—8 stitches. Work 11 rows even. Shape top as for little finger.
Middle Finger
Place remaining 6 stitches from holder onto needle, ready to work a RS row. Cut F.
Next row (RS) With C, k1, loop cast

on 1 stitch, k4, loop cast on 1 stitch, k1—8 stitches. Work 13 rows even. Shape top as for index finger.
Thumb
With RS facing and E, begin at thumb bind-off and pick up and knit 10 stitches along edge of thumb base (see Right Glove diagram).
Row 1 (WS) Purl.
Row 2 K1, M1, k6, k2tog, k1.
Rows 3–8 Repeat Rows 1 and 2 three times.
Row 9 Purl.
Row 10 [K2tog] 5 times—5 stitches.
Row 11 P2tog, p1, p2tog. Bind off remaining 3 stitches. Fold cuff in half and sew bound-off edge to WS. With crochet hook and 1 strand MC, work slip stitch in every stitch around edge of glove, omitting lower edge of cuff.

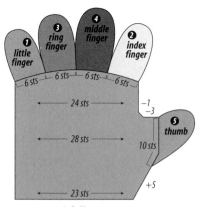

Left Glove

Left Glove Pocket

Work cuff as for right glove pocket.

Shape palm and base of thumb

Pick up stitches as for right glove pocket.

Row 1 (WS) Purl.

Row 2 K1, M1, knit to end.

Rows 3–10 Repeat Rows 1 and 2 four times—28 stitches. Work 5 rows even.

Next row (RS) Bind off 3 stitches, knit to end—25 stitches.

Next row Purl to last 2 stitches, p2tog—24 stitches (thumb base complete). Work 8 rows even.

Shape fingers

Little Finger

Next row (RS) K18 and place these stitches on hold. With A, work last 6 stitches as follows: K1, loop cast on 1 stitch, k4, loop cast on 1 stitch, k1—8 stitches. Work 9 rows even. Shape top as for right index finger.

Index Finger

Place 18 stitches from holder onto needle, ready to work a WS row.

Next row (WS) With F, p12 and place these stitches on hold. With D, work last 6 stitches as follows: P1, loop cast on 1 stitch, p4, loop cast on 1 stitch, p1—8 stitches. Work 11 rows even. Shape top as for right little finger.

Ring Finger

Place 12 sts from holder onto needle, ready to work a RS row.

Next row (RS) With F, k6 and place these stitches on hold. With B, work last 6 stitches as follows: K1, loop cast on 1 stitch, k4, loop cast on 1 stitch, k1—8 stitches. Work 11 rows even. Shape top as for right index finger.

Middle Finger

Place remaining 6 stitches from holder onto needle, ready to work a WS row. Cut F.

Next row (WS) With C, p1, loop cast on 1 stitch, p4, loop cast on 1 stitch, p1—8 stitches. Work 13 rows even. Shape top as for right little finger.

Thumb

With RS facing and E, pick up and knit 10 stitches along edge of thumb base to correspond to right thumb. Work as for right thumb, except work Row 2 as follows:

Row 2 K1, SSK, k6, M1, k1.

Complete as for right pocket.

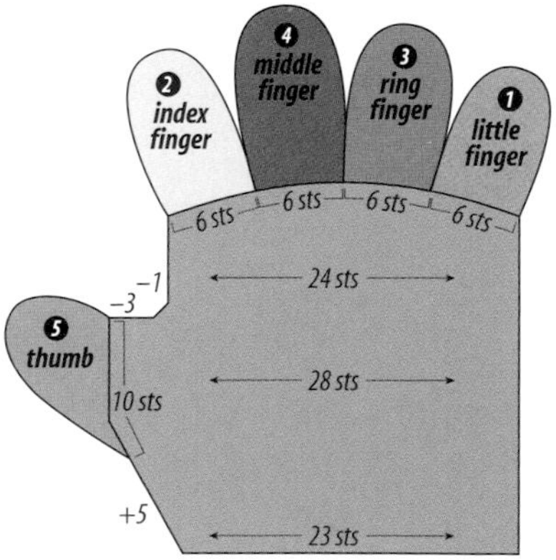

Finishing

Block pieces. Using photo as guide, pin pockets to fronts, then sew in place (sewing through slip stitch edging). Join shoulders, using 3-needle bind-off.

Buttonband

(**Note** Work all bands with 5mm/ US8 needles and 2 strands of MC.) Place 7 left front band stitches onto needle, ready to work a RS row.

Row 1 (RS) M1 (selvage stitch), [k1, p1] 3 times, k1—8 stitches. Continue in rib pattern until band, when slightly stretched, fits along front edge to neck, end with a WS row. Place stitches on hold. Sew band in place.

Buttonhole band

Place 4 markers along right front edge for buttonholes, with the first approximately 2¾ (3, 3, 3¼)" below neck edge, and 3 others spaced evenly between first marker and buttonhole at lower edge. Place 7 right front band stitches onto needle, ready to work a WS row.

Row 1 (WS) M1 (selvage stitch), [p1, k1] 3 times, p1—8 stitches. Complete to correspond to buttonband, working buttonholes as before at markers. End with a WS row. Do not cut yarn.

Right Glove

Labels in diagram:
❷ index finger
❹ middle finger
❸ ring finger
❶ little finger
❺ thumb
6 sts, 6 sts, 6 sts, 6 sts
24 sts
–1
–3
28 sts
10 sts
+5
23 sts

Neckband

Row 1 (RS) Rib 6, SSK, then pick up and knit 55 (59, 65, 65) stitches evenly around neck edge, work across button band stitches as follows: k2tog, rib to end—69 (73, 79, 79) stitches.

Row 2 *P1, k1; repeat from*, end p1. Work in rib pattern for 4 rows more, working buttonhole on next RS row. Bind off in rib. Sew top of sleeves to straight edges of armholes. Sew 1¼" portion at top of sleeves (above markers) to bound-off armhole stitches. Sew side and sleeve seams. Sew on buttons.

BOY'S MITTEN VERSION

Back and Fronts

Work as for Glove Pocket Version with the following changes: cast on and work ribbing with A, working buttonhole row on left front instead of right front; work stockinette stitch portion with MC.

Sleeves

Work as for Glove Pocket Version in the following colors: Cast on and work ribbing with A. Work Stripe Pattern as follows: *Work 2 rows each with A, B, MC, B; repeat from* (8 rows).

Left Mitten Pocket

(**Note** Work mittens with single strand of yarn.)

Work cuff

With size 3.25mm/US3 needles and A, cast on 26 stitches.

Begin Stripe Pattern: Row 1 (RS) Knit across: [2A, 2B, 2MC] 4 times, 2A.

Row 2 Purl, matching colors.

Rows 3–8 Repeat Rows 1 and 2 three times. Change to 2.75mm/US2 needles.

Work body

Next row (RS) With A, knit, increasing 3 stitches evenly across—29 stitches. Work 2 rows even with A.

Begin Chart A: Row 1 (WS) P7, place marker (pm), work row 1 of Chart A over 15 stitches, pm, p7. Continue in pattern, working chart between markers, and remaining stitches with A, through chart row 39. Continue with A, binding off 2 stitches at beginning of next 4 rows. Bind off remaining 21 stitches.

Work thumb

With RS facing and A, begin 1½" above cuff and pick up and knit 10 stitches along right edge of mitten.

Row 1 (WS) Purl.

Row 2 K1, SSK, k6, M1, k1.

Rows 3–10 Repeat Rows 1 and 2 four times.

Row 11 Purl.

Row 12 [K2tog] 5 times—5 stitches. Bind off. With crochet hook and 2 strands A, work slip stitch in every other stitch around edge of mitten, omitting lower edge of cuff. With MC, make 1" pompon for tail and attach to pocket, using photo as guide.

Right Mitten Pocket

Work cuff as for left mitten pocket.

Work body

Work as for left mitten pocket, working 9 rows of Chart B in place of first 9 rows of Chart A, then continue with Chart A from row 10.

Work thumb

With RS facing and A, pick up and knit 10 stitches along left edge of mitten to correspond to left mitten pocket. Work as for left thumb, except work Row 2 as follows:

Row 2 K1, M1, k6, k2tog, k1. Complete as for left pocket.

Finishing

Work as for Glove Pocket Version, working front and neck bands with A and reversing buttonhole and button bands.

SLIP STITCH CROCHET ————

1 Insert the hook into a stitch, catch yarn, and pull up a loop.

2 Insert hook into the next stitch to the left, catch yarn and pull through both the stitch and the loop on the hook; 1 loop on hook. Repeat Step 2.

Chart A · Left Mitten

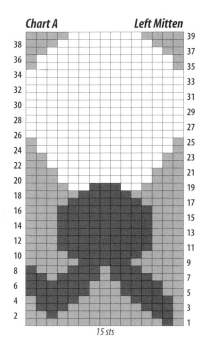

15 sts

Chart B · Right Mitten

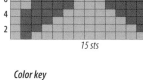

15 sts

Color key
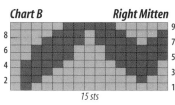
- ■ MC
- ▨ A
- □ B

Note: Reverse ears of right mitten by working Chart B in place of first 9 rows of Chart A, then continue with Chart A from row 10.

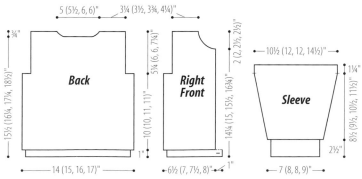

Back

5 (5½, 6, 6)" 3¼ (3½, 3¾, 4¼)"

¾"

5¼ (6, 6, 7¼)"

15½ (16¼, 17¼, 18½)"

10 (10, 11, 11)"

1"

14 (15, 16, 17)"

Right Front

2 (2, 2½, 2½)"

14¼ (15, 15½, 16¾)"

1"

6½ (7, 7½, 8)" 1"

Sleeve

10½ (12, 12, 14½)"

1¼"

8½ (9½, 10½, 11½)"

2½"

7 (8, 8, 9)"

53

12

Knit a kid's sweater with year-round appeal. Eight interchangeable panels celebrate special times in a small child's life. A sunny summer smile, a Valentine heart, and other motifs are as fun to knit as they are to wear.

Designed by Bonnie Franz

Celebration Pullover

INTERMEDIATE

STANDARD FIT

2 (4, 8, 10)
A 26 (28, 32, 34)"
B 14 (15½, 17, 18)"
C 15½ (17, 19, 20½)"

10cm/4"

28

21

• over stockinette stitch (knit on RS, purl on WS) using larger needles

1 2 3 **4** 5 6

• Medium weight
MC • 450 (540, 665, 750) yds
A–G • small amounts of each

• 3.5mm/US4 and 4mm/US6
or size to obtain gauge

3.5mm/US4, 40cm/16" long

• ten 20mm/¾"

• yarn needle & stitch markers

Note
See *Techniques*, page 80, for SSK and intarsia knitting.

Back
With smaller needles and MC, cast on 67 (73, 83, 89) stitches. Work in k1, p1 rib for 8 rows, increasing 1 stitch on last row—68 (74, 84, 90) stitches. Change to larger needles. Work in stockinette stitch until piece measures 14 (15½, 17, 18)" from beginning. Bind off.

Front
Work as for back until piece measures 12 (13½, 15, 16)" from beginning, end with a WS row.
Shape neck
Next row (RS) K29 (30, 35, 37), join 2nd ball of yarn and bind off 10 (14, 14, 16) stitches, knit to end. Working both sides at same time, bind off from each neck edge 3 stitches once, 2 stitches twice, 1 stitch twice—20 (21, 26, 28) stitches each side. Work even until piece measures same length as back to shoulder. Bind off.

Sleeves
With smaller needles and MC, cast on 35 (37, 41, 43) stitches. Work in k1, p1 rib for 8 rows, increasing 1 stitch on last row—36 (38, 42, 44) stitches. Change to larger needles. Work in stockinette stitch, increasing 1 stitch each side on 3rd (3rd, 5th, 5th) row, then every 4th (2nd, 4th, 4th) row 12 (1, 15, 9) times more, then every 0 (4th, 0, 6th) row 0 (13, 0, 5) times—62 (68, 74, 74) stitches. Work even until piece measures 9 (10, 11, 12)" from beginning. Bind off.

Finishing
Block pieces. Sew shoulders.
Neckband
With RS facing, circular needle and MC, begin at left shoulder and pick up and knit 38 (42, 42, 44) stitches evenly along front neck, and 28 (32, 32, 34) stitches along back neck—66 (74, 74, 78) stitches. Place marker, join and work k1, p1 rib in rounds for 1". Bind off.
Place markers 6 (6½, 7, 7)" down from shoulders on front and back for

Size 2 TAHKI/STACY CHARLES Cotton Classic (cotton; 50g; 108 yds) in 3856 (MC), 3488 (A), 3001 (B), 3559 (C), 3725 (D), 3769 (E), 3861 (F), 3331 (G)

armholes. Sew top of sleeves between markers. Sew side and sleeve seams. Sew buttons for panel on front, following schematic for placement.

Panel (make 1 for each motif desired)

With smaller needles and MC, cast on 47 stitches.

Begin Panel Chart: Row 1 (RS) *K1, p1; repeat from*, end k1.

Row 2 *P1, k1; repeat from*, end p1.

Row 3 K1, p1, SSK, yo, [k1, p1] 6 times, SSK, yo, [k1, p1] 5 times, SSK, yo, [k1, p1] 6 times, SSK, yo, k1, p1, k1.

Rows 4, 6, and 8 Repeat Row 2.

Rows 5 and 7 Repeat Row 1.

Begin Motif: Row 9 With MC, [k1, p1] twice, knit 39 stitches of desired motif, then with MC, [p1, k1] twice.

Row 10 With MC, [p1, k1] twice, purl 39 stitches of motif, then with MC, [k1, p1] twice.

Rows 11–20 Repeat Rows 9 and 10 five times.

Row 21 With MC, k1, p1, SSK, yo, knit 39 stitches of motif, with MC, yo, k2tog, p1, k1.

Row 22 Repeat Row 10.

Rows 23–36 Repeat Rows 9 and 10 seven times. Continue with MC only.

Row 37 [K1, p1] twice, k39, [p1, k1] twice.

Row 38 Repeat Row 2.

Rows 39–44 Repeat Rows 1–6.

Bind off. Work embroidery as necessary.

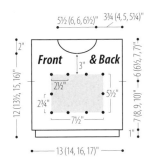

Chart Notes

1 Work MC section at left side of panel with a 2nd ball of MC when separated from right side of panel by a large area of contrasting motif color.

2 Work small areas of color on charts in duplicate stitch after panel is complete.

Duplicate stitch

Duplicate stitch (also known as Swiss darning) is just that: with a blunt tapestry needle threaded with a length of yarn of a contrasting color, cover a knitted stitch with an embroidered stitch of the same shape.

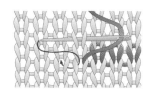

Birthday Cake

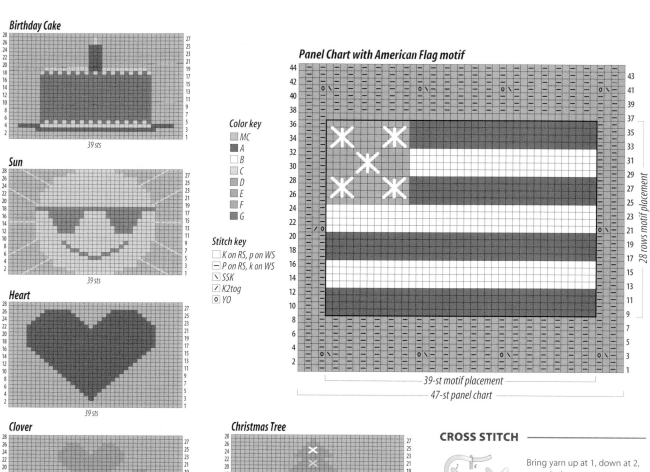

39 sts

Sun

39 sts

Heart

39 sts

Clover

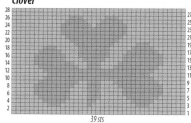

39 sts

Apple/Books

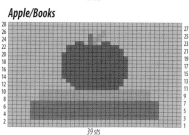

39 sts

Christmas Tree

39 sts

Pumpkin

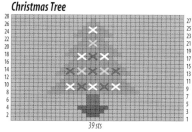

39 sts

Panel Chart with American Flag motif

39-st motif placement

47-st panel chart

28 rows motif placement

Color key
- ▨ MC
- ▨ A
- ▢ B
- ▨ C
- ▨ D
- ▨ E
- ▨ F
- ▨ G

Stitch key
- ▢ K on RS, p on WS
- ▬ P on RS, k on WS
- ◣ SSK
- ◢ K2tog
- ◯ YO

CROSS STITCH

Bring yarn up at 1, down at 2, up at 3, down at 4.

STAR STITCH

Work Steps 1-4 as above, then bring yarn up at 5, down at 6.

STRAIGHT STITCH

Bring yarn up at 1, down at 2, then up at 3.

57

Here is a traditional jacket in untraditional, yet sophisticated colors for a child. Use an easy-care light weight yarn that can be worn and easily cleaned for the next wear.

Designed by Celeste Pinheiro

Danish Nursery Jacket

INTERMEDIATE

LOOSE FIT

2 (4, 8, 10)
A 28½ (31, 34¾, 36½)"
B 12 (13, 13½, 15)"
C 15½ (17, 18, 18½)"

10cm/4"

25½, 28

22, 21
• over stockinette stitch (knit on RS, purl on WS) using larger needles
• over Chart Pattern using larger needles

1 2 **3** 4 5 6

• Light weight
MC • 400 (470, 530, 600) yds
CC • 270 (315, 355, 400) yds

• 3.5mm/US4 and 4mm/US6,
or size to obtain gauge

• five 1½" clasps

&
• stitch markers

Back
With smaller needles and MC, cast on 77 (85, 95, 99) stitches. Knit 9 rows. Change to larger needles. Beginning and ending as indicated for back, work in Chart Pattern until piece measures 11½ (12½, 13, 14½)" from beginning, end with a WS row.
Shape neck
Next row (RS) Work 24 (28, 32, 34) stitches, join 2nd ball of yarn and bind off center 29 (29, 31, 31) stitches, work to end. Working both sides at same time, decrease 1 stitch at each neck edge on next RS row—23 (27, 31, 33) stitches each side. Work 1 row even. Piece measures 12 (13, 13½, 15)" from beginning. Bind off all stitches.

Left Front
With smaller needles and MC, cast on 35 (39, 44, 46) stitches. Knit 9 rows. Change to larger needles. Beginning and ending as indicated for left front, work in Chart Pattern until piece measures 10½ (11½, 12, 13½)" from beginning, end with a RS row.

Shape neck
Next row (WS) Bind off 5 stitches (neck edge), work to end. Continue to bind off at neck edge at beginning of every WS row 3 stitches 1 (1, 2, 2) times, 2 stitches 2 (2, 1, 1) times—23 (27, 31, 33) stitches. Work even until piece measures same length as back to shoulder. Bind off all stitches.

Right Front
Work to correspond to left front, beginning and ending chart as indicated for right front. Reverse neck shaping by binding off at beginning of RS rows.

Sleeves
With smaller needles and MC, cast on 45 (47, 50, 53) stitches. Knit 9 rows. Change to larger needles and stockinette stitch. Work *4 rows CC, 4 rows MC; repeat from* for stripe pattern, AT SAME TIME, increase 1 stitch each side every 4th row 4 (0, 0, 0) times, every 6th row 5 (8, 9, 9) times—63 (63, 68, 71) stitches. Work even until piece measures 8½ (9, 9½, 9½)" from beginning. Bind off all stitches.

Finishing

Block pieces. Sew shoulder seams.
Place markers 6 (6, 6½, 6¾)" down from
shoulders on front and back for armholes.
Sew top of sleeves between markers. Sew
side and sleeve seams.

Neckband

With RS facing, smaller needles and MC,
begin at right front neck and pick up and
knit 68 (68, 72, 72) stitches evenly around
neck edge. Knit 9 rows. Bind off.

Front bands

With RS facing, smaller needles and MC,
pick up and knit 71 (77, 80, 89) stitches
evenly along each front edge. Knit 7
rows. Bind off all stitches. Using photo
as guide, sew 5 clasps to bands, the first
just below neckband, the last just above
lower edge band, and 3 others spaced
evenly between.

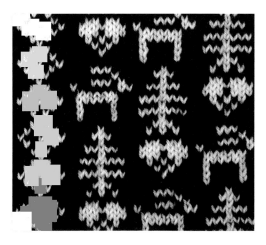

Size 8 PATONS Astra (acrylic; 50g; 178 yds)
in 2765 (MC) and 2783 (CC)

Chart Pattern

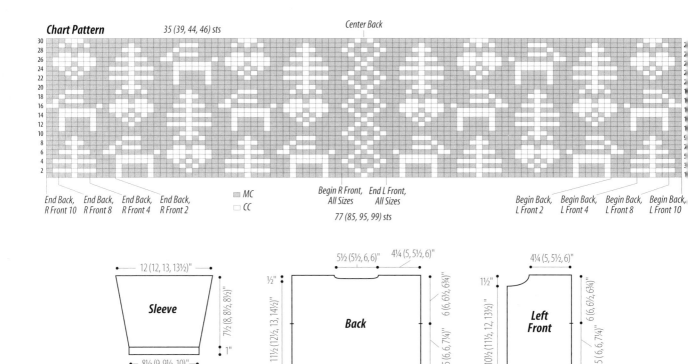

35 (39, 44, 46) sts

Center Back

30 28 26 24 22 20 18 16 14 12 10 8 6 4 2

End Back, R Front 10   End Back, R Front 8   End Back, R Front 4   End Back, R Front 2

■ MC
□ CC

Begin R Front, All Sizes   End L Front, All Sizes

77 (85, 95, 99) sts

Begin Back, L Front 2   Begin Back, L Front 4   Begin Back, L Front 8   Begin Back, L Front 10

Sleeve

12 (12, 13, 13½)"
7½ (8, 8½, 8½)"
8½ (9, 9½, 10)"
½"
1"

Back

5½ (5½, 6, 6)"   4¼ (5, 5½, 6)"
11½ (12½, 13, 14½)"
6 (6, 6½, 6¾)"
5 (6, 6, 7¼)"
14 (15½, 17¼, 18)"
1"

Left Front

4¼ (5, 5½, 6)"
1½"
10½ (11½, 12, 13½)"
6 (6, 6½, 6¾)"
5 (6, 6, 7¼)"
6½ (7, 8, 8½)"
1"

WEAVING THE CARRIES

The carried yarn is woven alternately above and below the working yarn on the purl side of the work.

To weave the carry above a purl stitch: Insert needle into stitch and under woven yarn, then purl the stitch as usual.

To weave the carry below a purl stitch: Insert needle into stitch and over woven yarn, then purl the stitch as usual.

Activity **14**
Sweater

Children like learning when it's fun, and we've got a sweater that's sure to entertain them while they practice with ties, snaps, buttons, and zippers. This colorful sweater is meant to be worn and enjoyed, so make it a bit larger to extend its wearing time.

Designed by Knitter's Design Team

Activity Sweater

INTERMEDIATE

LOOSE FIT

4 (6/8, 10)
A 29 (31, 34½)"
B 14¼ (16, 17½)"
C 16 (17½, 18½)"

10cm/4"

24
18

• over stockinette stitch (knit on RS, purl on WS) using larger needles

1 2 3 5 6

• Medium weight
A • 200 (240, 270) yds
B, D, & F • 65 (85, 100) yds each
C 95 • (105, 120) yds
E 75 • (85, 100) yds

• 4mm/US6 and 5mm/US8,
or size to obtain gauge

• three 25mm/1"

Notes

1 See *Techniques*, page 80, for SSK, SSP, yo before a knit and purl stitch, and intarsia knitting. **2** At color changes, bring new color under old color to twist yarns and prevent holes. **3** Follow charts for color placement. **4** Separate the zippers and switch colors for a 2-color zipper. After sewing in zipper, the extended area below the opening will be secured and cut off.

Back

With smaller needles and B, cast on 31 (33, 37) stitches, then with A, cast on an additional 31 (33, 37) stitches—62 (66, 74) stitches.
Begin Rib Pattern: Row 1 (RS) *P2, k2; repeat from* (changing colors in center), end p2. Work rib pattern as established for 11 (13, 13) rows more. Change to larger needles.
Next row (RS) Knit, increasing 2 stitches in each color section—33 (35, 39) stitches in each color section. Continue in

• stitch holder
• four snaps
• two 7" separating zippers in different colors

stockinette stitch (St st), matching colors, for 11 (13, 13) rows more.
Next row (RS) With A, knit to center of row, change to C and knit to end. Continue in pattern for 17 (19, 21) rows more. Continue to follow chart for color placement to armhole shaping. Piece measures approximately 8½ (9¾, 10½)" from beginning.
Shape armholes
Next row (RS) With E, bind off 7 (7, 9) stitches, knit to center of row, then with B, knit to end.
Next row With B, bind off 7 (7, 9) stitches, purl to end, matching colors—26 (28, 30) stitches in each color section. Work 4 (8, 12) more rows, matching colors. Then continue to follow chart for color placement to shoulders. Armhole measures approximately 5¾ (6¼, 7)". Bind off.

Front

Work as for back to armhole shaping.
Shape armholes and separate for zipper
Next row (RS) With E, bind off 7 (7, 9) stitches, knit to center, then with B, knit to end of row (without joining stitches at center).

Size 4 MISSION FALLS 1824 Wool (wool; 50g; 85 yds) in 013 (A), 026 (B), 023 (C), 011 (D), 027 (E), and 002 (F)

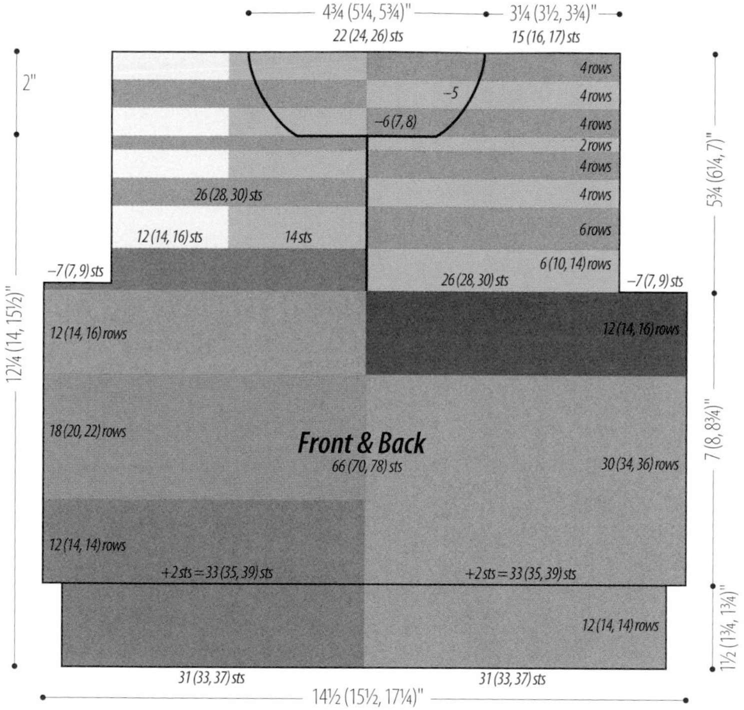
4¾ (5¼, 5¾)"
22 (24, 26) sts
3¼ (3½, 3¾)"
15 (16, 17) sts
2"
4 rows
-5
4 rows
-6 (7, 8)
4 rows
2 rows
4 rows
26 (28, 30) sts
4 rows
12 (14, 16) sts
14 sts
6 rows
6 (10, 14) rows
-7 (7, 9) sts
26 (28, 30) sts
-7 (7, 9) sts
5¾ (6¼, 7)"
12¼ (14, 15½)"
12 (14, 16) rows
12 (14, 16) rows
18 (20, 22) rows
Front & Back
66 (70, 78) sts
30 (34, 36) rows
7 (8, 8¾)"
12 (14, 14) rows
+2 sts = 33 (35, 39) sts
+2 sts = 33 (35, 39) sts
12 (14, 14) rows
1½ (1¾, 1¾)"
31 (33, 37) sts
31 (33, 37) sts
14½ (15½, 17¼)"

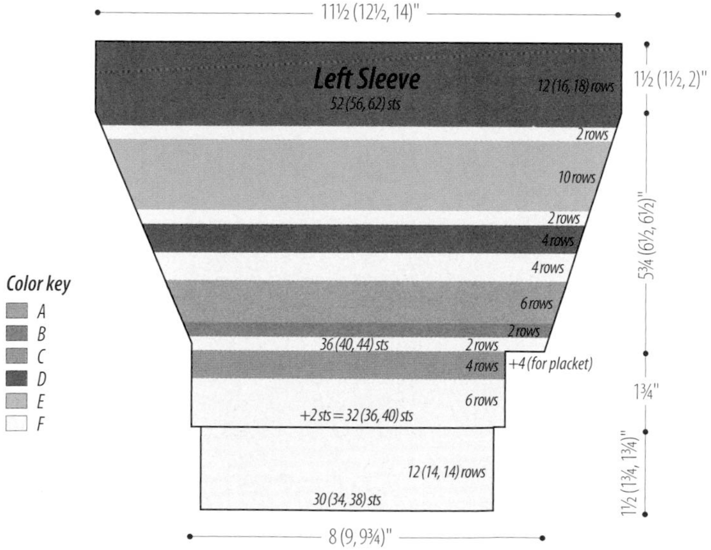
11½ (12½, 14)"
Left Sleeve
52 (56, 62) sts
12 (16, 18) rows
1½ (1½, 2)"
2 rows
10 rows
2 rows
4 rows
4 rows
6 rows
2 rows
5¾ (6½, 6½)"
36 (40, 44) sts
2 rows
4 rows
+4 (for placket)
1¾"
6 rows
+2 sts = 32 (36, 40) sts
12 (14, 14) rows
30 (34, 38) sts
1½ (1¾, 1¾)"
8 (9, 9¾)"
Color key
A
B
C
D
E
F

Next row With B, bind off 7 (7, 9) stitches, purl to end of right front, then with E, purl to end of left front. Working both sides at same time, work 20 (24, 28) rows more in pattern. Armhole measures approximately 3¾ (4¼, 5)".

Shape left front neck

Next row (RS) With A, knit to center and place remaining stitches on hold.

Next row (WS) Bind off 6 (7, 8) stitches, purl to end.

Next (decrease) row (RS) Knit to last 3 stitches, SSK, k1. Repeat decrease row every RS row 4 times more—15 (16, 17) stitches. Work 1 row even. Bind off.

Shape right front neck

Place stitches from holder on needle, ready to work a RS row.

Next row (RS) With E, bind off 6 (7, 8) stitches, knit in color pattern to end. Work 1 row even.

Next (decrease) row (RS) With E, k1, k2tog, knit in color pattern to end. Continue to work to correspond to left front neck.

Left Sleeve

With smaller needles and F, cast on 30 (34, 38) stitches. Work in k2, p2 rib for 12 (14, 14) rows. Change to larger needles.

Next row Knit, increasing 2 sts across—32 (36, 40) stitches. Work in St st for 5 rows more. With C, work 3 rows.

Shape placket

Next row (WS) With C, purl to end, cast on 4 stitches (for placket)—36 (40, 44) stitches. With F, work 2 rows. Continue following chart for left sleeve, AT SAME TIME, increase 1 stitch each side on next row, then every 4th row 5 (3, 6) times, every

6th row 2 (4, 2) times—52 (56, 62) stitches. Piece measures approximately 9 (10, 10)" from beginning. Work even until last row of chart has been worked. Piece measures approximately 10½ (11½, 12)" from beginning. Bind off.

Right Sleeve

Work to correspond to left sleeve, following Right Sleeve Chart for color placement. Reverse cuff placket shaping by casting on 4 stitches at end of 11th St st row above ribbing (a RS row).

Finishing

Block pieces. Sew shoulders. Sew top of sleeves to straight edges of armholes. Sew straight portion at top of sleeves to bound-off armhole stitches. Sew side seams of body from above ribbing to underarm, then sew sleeve seams, leaving plackets open.

Zipper opening trim

With RS facing, smaller needles and C, pick up and k18 (20, 22) stitches along left front edge of zipper opening, 2 stitches at bottom, and 18 (20, 22) stitches along right front edge—38 (42, 46) stitches.
Row 1 (WS) K17 (19, 21), SSK,

k2tog, k17 (19, 21). Bind off purlwise on next row.

Right sleeve cuff placket

With RS facing, smaller needles and C, pick up and knit 17 (18, 18) stitches along placket edge. Knit 5 rows. Bind off. Sew side of placket to cast-on placket stitches. Work other side of placket to correspond. Overlap first side over 2nd side and sew in place at top of placket.

Left sleeve cuff placket

Work as for right sleeve.

Pocket

With larger needles and F, cast on 28 stitches. Work in St st for 20 (24, 28) rows. Then work in rib pattern as follows:
Row 1 (RS) K3, *p2, k2; repeat from*, end p2, k3.
Row 2 P3, *k2, p2; repeat from*, end k2, p3.
Rows 3 and 4 Repeat rows 1 and 2.
Row 5 (buttonhole row) (RS) Rib 7, yo, p2tog, rib 3, SSP, yo, p2tog, rib 3, SSP, yo, rib 7.
Row 6 Work in rib pattern, working 2 stitches into center yo.
Rows 7–10 Work in rib pattern. Bind off loosely.

Visit knittinguniverse.com to design your own color scheme with Knitter's Paintbox.

Side ties (make 2)

With smaller needles and C, cast on 3 stitches. Work in St st for 60 rows. Bind off. Sew tie around side vent (see illustration on next page).

Neckband

With RS facing, smaller needles and C, pick up and knit 58 (62, 66) stitches evenly around neck edge (not including zipper trim).
Next row (WS) P2, *k2, p2; repeat from*. Work 6 rows more in rib pattern. Bind off in pattern. Center pocket on front, aligning bottom just above the rib, and sew in place. Sew buttons on body of sweater to correspond to buttonholes. Sew zipper into opening, following instructions on next page. Add 2 press-on snaps to each cuff placket, ½" and 1½" from cast-on.

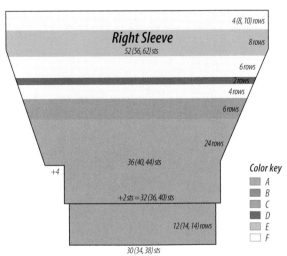

Right Sleeve
52 (56, 62) sts
4 (8, 10) rows
8 rows
6 rows
2 rows
4 rows
6 rows
24 rows
36 (40, 44) sts
+4
+2 sts = 32 (36, 40) sts
12 (14, 14) rows
30 (34, 38) sts

Color key
A
B
C
D
E
F

Zipping Along

Although knitted fabric has stretch, a zipper does not, and the two must be joined as neatly as possible to prevent ripples. Here are the steps to follow for smooth zipper placement.

1 Measure the length of the opening. Select a zipper in the color of your choice that matches the length of the opening. If you can't find one in that length, choose one that is a bit longer; the extra length will be dealt with in a later step.

2 Pre-shrink your zipper in the method you will use to clean the garment. Wash or carefully steam it. (You don't want to melt plastic or nylon teeth.)

3 Place the garment flat, making sure that each side matches up perfectly.

4 To fit a neckline opening, align the bottoms to the hem, allowing the extra to extend beyond the neck edge of the opening (4a), or match the top teeth to the top of the opening, allowing the extra length to extend below the bottom of the opening (4b).

5 Pin the zipper in place. Be generous with the pins, and take all the time you need. Extra care taken here makes the next steps easier.

6 Fold the extra fabric of the top zipper extension forward and outward from the center at right angles, and secure with pins.

7 Baste the zipper in place. When you are satisfied with the placement, remove the pins.

8 Pick in (sew in) the zipper, making neat, even stitches that should be firm enough to withstand the stress of wearing.

9 If the zipper extends beyond the lower opening of the neck, sew a new stop to secure the lower teeth together, and clip off the extra about a half-inch from the sewn stop. If the extra was at the top, clip it off as well.

10 Reinforce stress points at the top and bottom edges. Your zippered garment is now ready to wear.

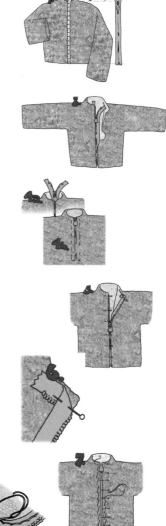

SEWING ON TIES

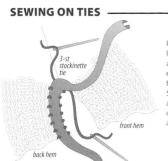

3-st stockinette tie

front hem

back hem

Fold tie in half lengthwise. Center tie at top of vent, allowing extra to extend at bottom edges for ties. Sew both edges of tie around vent, as shown, covering 2 purl stitches at each side.

65

This is the best of all knits for a little princess—fun, simple, and cropped. Smooth stockinette with easy shaping is accented with clever knotted I-cord.

Designed by Megan Lacey

Knitted Knotted

EASY +

LOOSE FIT

2 (4, 6)
A 27 (31, 35)"
B 11 (12, 14)"
C 14½ (16, 18)"

10cm/4"

28 [grid] 20

• over stockinette stitch using MC (knit on RS, purl on WS)

 1 2 3 **4** 5 6

• Medium weight
MC • 460 (560, 720) yds
CC • 120 yds

[needles]

• 5mm/US8,
or size to obtain gauge

• 5mm/US8, 40cm/16" long

[needles]

• two 5mm/US8

 &

• stitch markers and holders

Note

See *Techniques*, page 80, for 3-needle bind-off and unattached I-cord.

Back

With MC, cast on 67 (77, 87) stitches. Beginning with a knit row, work 36 (38, 46) rows in stockinette stitch (St st). Piece measures approximately 5 (5½, 6½)". Place marker (pm) each side of row for underarm. Work 40 (44, 50) rows even. Cut MC. Change to CC and knit 2 rows. Armhole measures approximately 6 (6½, 7½)" above markers. Place stitches on hold.

Front

Work as for back until there are 20 (22, 26) rows above armhole markers and armhole measures approximately 2¾ (3, 3¾)".

Shape neck

Next row (RS) Knit 26 (31, 36), join 2nd ball of yarn and bind off center 15 stitches, knit to end. Working both sides at same time, decrease 1 stitch at each neck edge every RS row 5 times—21 (26, 31) stitches each side. Work even until armhole measures same length as back to shoulder, ending with 2 CC rows. Place stitches on hold.

Sleeves

With MC, cast on 40 (42, 42) stitches. Work in St st, increasing 1 stitch each side on 5th (5th, 3rd) row, then every 4th (4th, 2nd) row 6 (7, 3) times, then every 6th (6th, 4th) row 3 (3, 12) times—60 (64, 74) stitches. Work 3 rows even. Cut MC. Change to CC and knit 2 rows, purl 1 row. Piece measures approximately 7½ (8, 9)" from beginning. Bind off.

Finishing

With CC, join shoulders, using 3-needle bind-off as follows: With RS of front and back together, join 21 (26, 31) stitches of one shoulder, bind off back neck stitches until 21 (26, 31) stitches remain, join other shoulder.

Neckband

With RS facing, circular needle and CC, begin at left shoulder and pick up and

Size 2 PLYMOUTH YARN Outback (wool; 100g; 230 yds) in 906 (MC); Galway (wool; 200g; 370 yds) in 107 (CC)

knit 70 (74, 78) stitches evenly around neck edge. Pm, join and purl 1 round. Cut CC. Change to MC and work 6 rounds in k1, p1 rib. Then knit every round for 1¼" more. Cut MC. With CC, knit 1 round. Bind off.

Sew top of sleeves between armhole markers of front and back. Sew side and sleeve seams.

Body I-cord trim

With dpns and CC, cast on 5 stitches. Work I-cord for 78 (90, 102)". Bind off. Tie 16 knots evenly spaced in cord and sew trim around lower edge of sweater. Sew ends of trim together.

Sleeve I-cord trim

Work I-cord for 24 (26, 26)". Bind off. Tie 6 knots in cord and sew around cuff edge. Sew ends of trim together.

I-CORD KNOTS

Tie I-cord into a knot.

Tie knots evenly spaced in I-cord.

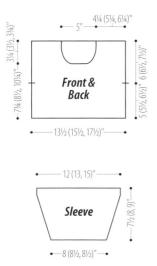

Front & Back

4¼ (5¼, 6¼)"

5"

3¼ (3½, 3¾)"

7¾ (8½, 10¼)"

6 (6½, 7½)"

5 (5½, 6½)"

13½ (15½, 17½)"

Sleeve

12 (13, 15)"

7½ (8, 9)"

8 (8½, 8½)"

Any little girl will fall for this soft pullover. Cross-stitch embroidery accents the large blocks of color. Use short lengths of mohair for the stitching to prevent tangles, or use a different yarn for added interest.

Designed by Diane Zangl

Checker Block

INTERMEDIATE

C
B | A
LOOSE FIT

2 (4, 6, 10, 12)
A 26½ (28½, 30, 34, 36)"
B 14¼ (15½, 18, 19¼, 21¼)"
C 18 (19½, 20, 24, 26)"

10cm/4"

20
13
• over stockinette stitch (knit on RS, purl on WS) using larger needles

1 2 3 **4** 5 6
Medium weight
A • 75 (90, 105, 135, 155) yds
B • 120 (140, 160, 205, 240) yds
C • 130 (150, 170, 205, 240) yds

• 5mm/US8 and 5.5mm/US9,
or size to obtain gauge

5mm/US8, 40cm/16" long

&
• yarn needle
• stitch marker

Note
1 See *Techniques*, page 80, for intarsia knitting. **2** Bring new color under old at color changes to prevent holes.

Color Block Diagram

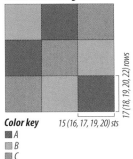

Color key   15 (16, 17, 19, 20) sts
17 (18, 19, 20, 22) rows
■ *A*
■ *B*
■ *C*

K2, P2 Rib (multiple of 4 stitches, plus 2)
Row 1 (RS) *K2, p2; repeat from*, end k2.
Row 2 *P2, k2; repeat from*, end p2.

Back
With smaller needles and A, cast on 42 (46, 50, 54, 58) stitches. Work in K2, P2 Rib for 1½", increasing 3 (2, 1, 3, 2) stitches evenly across last (WS) row—45 (48, 51, 57, 60) stitches. Change to larger needles. Work in stockinette stitch and follow Color Block Diagram until piece measures 8¾ (9½, 11½, 12¾, 14)" from beginning, end with a WS row.
Shape armholes
Bind off 4 (5, 6, 7, 7) stitches at beginning of next 2 rows—37 (38, 39, 43, 46) stitches. Work even until armhole measures 4¼ (4¾, 5¼, 5¼, 6)", end with a WS row.
Shape neck
Next row (RS) Knit 12 (12, 12, 13, 14), join 2nd ball of yarn and bind off center 13 (14, 15, 17, 18) stitches, knit to end. Working both sides at same time, decrease 1 stitch at each neck edge every RS row twice—10 (10, 10, 11, 12) stitches each side. Work 1 row even. Armhole measures 5½ (6, 6½, 6½, 7¼)". Bind off.

Front
Work as for back until armhole measures 3½ (4, 4½, 4½, 5¼)", end with a WS row.
Shape neck
Next row (RS) K13 (13, 13, 14, 15), join 2nd ball of yarn and bind off center 11 (12,

Size 6 CLASSIC ELITE La Gran Mohair (mohair, wool, nylon; 42g; 90 yds) 6562 (A), 6539 (B), 6599 (C)

Visit knittinguniverse.com to design your own color scheme with **Knitter's Paintbox**.

13, 15, 16) stitches, knit to end. Working both sides at same time, decrease 1 stitch at each neck edge every RS row 3 times—10 (10, 10, 11, 12) stitches each side. Work even until armhole measures same length as back to shoulder. Bind off.

Left Sleeve
With smaller needles and A, cast on 22 (26, 26, 30, 30) stitches. Work in K2, P2 Rib for 2", end with a WS row. Change to larger needles and B. Work in stockinette stitch, increasing 1 stitch at each side on 3rd (5th, 5th, 7th, 5th) row, then every 6th (6th, 6th, 10th, 6th) row 7 (1, 8, 6, 2) times, then every 0 (8th, 0, 0, 8th) row 0 (5, 0, 0, 7) times—38 (40, 44, 44, 50) stitches. Work 1 row even. Sleeve measures approximately 11¼ (12½, 12¾, 15½, 16¾)" from beginning. Work 1¼ (1½, 1¾, 2¼, 2¼)" even. Bind off.

Right Sleeve
Work as for left sleeve, substituting color C for B.

Finishing
Block pieces. Sew shoulders.
Neckband
With RS facing, circular needle and C (C, C, A, A), begin at left shoulder and pick up and knit 30 (32, 32, 34, 34) stitches evenly along front neck, and 26 (28, 28, 30, 30) stitches along back

neck—56 (60, 60, 64, 64) stitches. Place marker, join and work k2, p2 rib as follows: **Round 1** *K2, p2; repeat from*. Repeat Round 1 until band measures 1". Bind off.

Embroidery
Using photo as guide, with yarn needle and double strand of desired colors, work cross stitch (see illustration) centered over join between color blocks. Sew top of sleeves to straight edges of armholes. Sew straight edge at top of sleeves to bound-off armhole stitches. Sew side and sleeve seams.

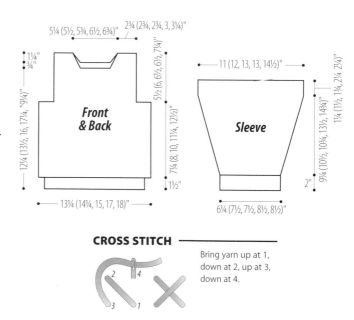

CROSS STITCH

Bring yarn up at 1, down at 2, up at 3, down at 4.

Sock knitting has enchanted many a knitter, and there may be knitters who think they've knit up just about every kind of sock—but we bet you haven't made a pair with pockets!

Designed by Julie Gaddy

Treasure Pocket Socks

INTERMEDIATE

Child 6–10 yrs

10cm/4"

37

27

• over stockinette stitch (knit every round)

 2 3 4 5 6

Super fine weight
MC • 200 yds
A–C • 2 yds for flaps
• 4 yds for pockets
• 25 yds for heels and toes

• four 2.75mm/US2, or size to obtain gauge

• two 8mm/⁵⁄₁₆"

Notes

1 See *Techniques*, page 80, for SSK, grafting, and working with double-pointed needles (dpns). *2* Slip stitches purlwise with yarn at WS of work.

Sock

With MC, cast on 54 stitches, divided evenly over 3 dpns (18/18/18). Join, being careful not to twist stitches.
Round 1 *K1, p1; repeat from*. Repeat Round 1 until piece measures 1½".
Next round *[K3, p2] twice, [k2, knit into front and back of next stitch, p1] twice; repeat from* twice more—60 stitches (20/20/20).
Next round *K3, p2; repeat from*. Repeat last round until piece measures 5½" from beginning.
Divide for heel
Next round Work to last 18 stitches of round, slip last 2 stitches worked onto center needle (20/22/18). Cut MC. With empty needle and A, work as follows over next 34 stitches: K4, [k2tog, k6] 3 times, k2tog, k4. Place 26 remaining MC stitches on hold for instep. Work back and forth in rows over 30 A stitches only.

Work heel flap
Row 1 (WS) Sl 1, purl to end.
Row 2 *Sl 1, k1; repeat from* to end.
Repeat last 2 rows 12 times more.
Turn heel
Row 1 (WS) Sl 1, p16, p2tog, p1, turn work, leaving remaining stitches unworked.
Row 2 (RS) Sl 1, k5, SSK, k1, turn.
Row 3 Sl 1, p6, p2tog, p1, turn.
Row 4 Sl 1, k7, SSK, k1, turn.
Row 5 Sl 1, p8, p2tog, p1, turn.
Row 6 Sl 1, k9, SSK, k1, turn.
Row 7 Sl 1, p10, p2tog, p1, turn.
Row 8 Sl 1, k11, SSK, k1, turn.
Row 9 Sl 1, p12, p2tog, p1, turn.
Row 10 Sl 1, k13, SSK, k1, turn.
Row 11 Sl 1, p14, p2tog, p1, turn.
Row 12 Sl 1, k15, SSK, k1—18 stitches.
Do not turn. Cut A.
Shape gusset
Divide work over 3 dpns as follows:
With empty needle (Needle 1) and MC, pick up and knit 15 stitches along side edge of heel flap, then with a 2nd needle (Needle 2), work in rib pattern as established across 26 instep stitches on hold; with a 3rd needle (Needle 3), pick up and knit 15 stitches along side edge of heel flap, then knit 9 heel stitches

from next needle, slip remaining 9 heel stitches onto Needle 1—(24/26/24). Work in rounds as follows:

Round 1 Knit across stitches of Needle 1; rib 26 from Needle 2; knit across stitches of Needle 3.

Round 2 Knit to last 3 stitches of Needle 1, k2tog, k1; rib 26 from Needle 2; from Needle 3, k1, SSK, knit to end. Repeat last 2 rounds 10 times more—52 stitches (13/26/13).

Work even until foot measures 1½" less than desired length from back of heel to end of toe. Cut MC. Continue with A only.

Shape toe

Round 1 Needle 1: knit to last 3 stitches, k2tog, k1; Needle 2: k1, SSK, knit to last 3 stitches, k2tog, k1; Needle 3: k1, SSK, knit to end.

Round 2 Knit. Repeat last 2 rounds 6 times more (6/12/6). With Needle 3, knit the stitches from Needle 1—12 stitches on each of 2 needles. Cut A, leaving a tail for grafting. Graft stitches together.

Pocket (make 2)

With B, cast on 10 stitches. Work 12 rows in stockinette stitch (knit on RS, purl on WS). Bind off.

Pocket flap (make 2)

With C, cast on 10 stitches.

Rows 1, 3 and 5 (WS) Purl.

Row 2 K1, k2tog, k4, SSK, k1—8 stitches.

Row 4 K1, k2tog, k1, yo, k1, SSK, k1—7 stitches.

Row 6 K1, k2tog, k1, SSK, k1—5 stitches.

Row 7 P2tog, p1, p2tog—3 stitches. Bind off.

Finishing

With A, beginning at upper right corner of pocket flap, work whip stitch around edge of flap to upper left corner (do not cut yarn), then whip stitch top of flap to pocket, centered on side of sock, approximately 3" below top of sock. Whip stitch 3 sides of pocket to sock, centered under flap. Take yarn to inside of sock and secure. Sew button on pocket. Block lightly.

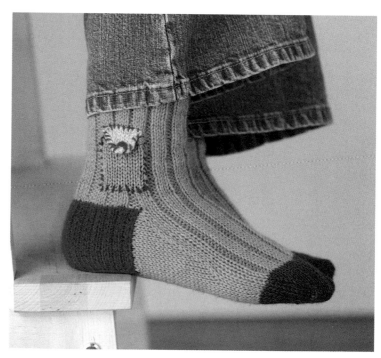

SKACEL Fortissima Socka Polycolon (wool, polycolon; 50g; 214 yds) in 1404 (MC), 1403 (A), 1408 (B), 1413 (C)

Start with a bunch of garter-stitch triangles, join them in a circle, and shape the top. Then comes the fun: applying I-cord everywhere for a hat with many personalities. Turn it inside out and get a staid cloche. Hook flaps to the loops on the top for wilder looks, or pull them down for extra warmth.

Designed by Lois Young

Jester Metamorphosis

INTERMEDIATE

One Size
Approximate circumference 18"

10cm/4"

50

22

• over Circular Garter Stitch

1 2 3 **4** 5 6

• Medium weight
MC • 200 yds
CC • 50 yds

• 3.5mm/US4, or size to obtain gauge, 40cm/16" long

• four 3.5mm/US4

&

• stitch holders and markers

Notes

1 See *Techniques*, page 80, for SSK, Make 1 (M1), and S2KP2. **2** Change to double-pointed needles (dpns) when necessary. **3** Slip stitches purlwise with yarn at WS of work. **4** For ease of working, mark RS of work.

Circular Garter Stitch

Round 1 Knit.
Round 2 Purl.
Repeat Rounds 1 and 2 for Circular Garter Stitch.

Unattached I-Cord

With dpn, cast on 3 stitches. *K3, do not turn, slide stitches to opposite end of needle; repeat from*.

Attached I-Cord

With dpn, cast on 3 stitches. K3, *pick up and knit 1 stitch through edge stitch or loop of stitch on garment, do not turn, slide stitches to opposite end of needle, k2, SSK; repeat from*.

Flaps (make 6)

With dpn and MC, cast on 2 stitches. Work back and forth in rows as follows:

Row 1 (WS) Knit.
Row 2 Slip 1, M1, k1.
Rows 3–5 Slip 1, knit to end.
Row 6 Slip 1, M1, knit to last stitch, M1, k1—5 stitches.
Repeat Rows 3–6 six times more—17 stitches. Work Rows 3–5 once more. Cut yarn and place stitches on hold.

Hat

With RS facing, place all flap stitches on circular needle with markers between flaps—102 stitches. Place a different color marker for beginning of round, join, and work in circular garter stitch for 5½", ending last round (a purl round) 1 stitch before round marker.

Shape crown

Next (decrease) round *Slip 1, remove marker, replace slipped stitch on left needle, replace marker (marker moved 1 stitch to the right), S2KP2, knit to 1 stitch before next marker; repeat from* around, end last repeat knit to marker—15 stitches between markers. Repeat decrease round every 4th round 7 times more—6 stitches. Cut yarn. Draw yarn through remaining stitches and secure.

Flap trim

With dpn and CC, begin between 2 flaps, *work Attached I-cord along edge of flap to point, work 11 rounds of Unattached I-cord, then begin in same stitch as last Attached I-cord round and work Attached I-cord along remaining edge of flap; repeat from* around. Fasten off. Sew ends of I-cord together.

Crown trim

Fold hat at 10th garter ridge above flaps. Baste in place. *Baste a CC thread from center point between 2 flaps through a column of stitches to top of crown; repeat from* around—6 basting lines. *With CC, work Attached I-cord along one basting line, attaching first stitch through loop of stitch on hat and through both thicknesses of flap trim. At top of hat, work 11 rounds Unattached I-cord for loop, attach I-cord to same stitch at base of loop, then to stitch at top of next basting line, work and attach another 11-round I-cord loop, then work Attached I-cord down basting line. Attach last stitch through both hat and flap trim. Work 1 round Unattached I-cord, k3tog, fasten off; repeat from* around. Remove basting.

TAHKI Limbo (superwash wool; 50g; 138 yds) in 4540 (MC) and 4518 (CC)

75

When you find a great motif, isn't it fun to expand its possibilities? Here we have a trio of kid-friendly, garter-stitch pieces, all using Lois' jovial sunny face: a pillow, a stuffed toy, and a handy bag. Make one, or better yet, why not make all three? We've made ours using yellow, red, and blue.

Designed by Lois Young

Sun Spots

EASY+

One Size
Stuffed Toy
Diameter 10"
Pillow and Bag
12" x 12"

10cm/4"
36
18
• over garter stitch (knit every row)

1 2 3 **4** 5 6
• Medium weight
MC • 800 yds
A & B • 200 yds each

• 5.5mm/US9, or size to obtain gauge

• two 5.5mm/US9

EYES• two 22mm/⅞"
NOSE• one 20mm/¾"
MOUTH• one 28mm/1⅛"

• fiber fill

Notes

1 See *Techniques*, page 80, for SSK and Make 1 (M1). **2** Slip the first stitch of every row purlwise, with yarn in front. **3** For ease in knitting, mark RS of work.

Attached I-cord

Row 1 Pick up and knit 1 stitch, as directed—4 stitches on needle. Do not turn. Slide stitches to opposite end of needle, k2, SSK. Repeat Row 1.

Unattached I-cord

Row 1 Do not turn, slide stitches to opposite end of needle, k3. Repeat Row 1.

Sun

Center

With MC, cast on 9 stitches.
Row 1 (WS) Slip 1, knit to end.
Row 2 Slip 1, knit into front and back of next stitch (kf&b), knit to last 2 stitches, kf&b, k1.
Repeat last 2 rows 8 times more—27 stitches. Knit 19 rows, slipping first stitch of every row.
Decrease row (RS) Slip 1, SSK, knit to last 3 stitches, k2tog, k1.

Next row Slip 1, knit to end.
Repeat last 2 rows 7 times more. Work decrease row once more—9 stitches. Bind off.

Triangle Points

Note Pick up and knit 11 stitches with RS of work facing as directed for each point, then work point as follows:
Row 1 (WS) Slip 1, SSK, knit to end.
Rows 2–8 Repeat Row 1.
Row 9 Slip 1, SSK.
Row 10 SSK. Fasten off last stitch.

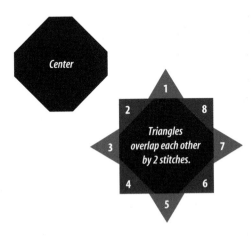

Center

1 2 8 3 7 4 6 5

Triangles overlap each other by 2 stitches.

PLYMOUTH Encore (acrylic, wool; 100g; 200 yds) in 174 (MC), 517 (A), and 848 (B)

POINT 1 With A, pick up and knit 11 stitches along bound-off edge, beginning 1 stitch before, and ending 1 stitch after 9 bound-off stitches.

POINT 2 With B, pick up and knit 2 stitches in front of Point 1, then pick up and knit 9 more stitches—11 stitches.

POINT 3 With A, pick up and knit 2 stitches behind Point 2, then pick up and knit 9 more stitches—11 stitches.

POINTS 4–8 Continue to work as for points 2 and 3, picking up last 2 stitches of Point 8 in front of Point 1.

Square

With MC, cast on 50 stitches.

Row 1 (WS) Slip 1, knit to end.

Repeat Row 1 until piece is square (approximately 50 garter ridges), end with a RS row. Bind off.

STUFFED TOY

Make 2 suns. Sew face buttons on one sun.

Join suns with I-cord edging

Place suns with WS together. With double-pointed needles (dpns) and MC, cast on 3 stitches. Begin at base of any triangle point and, picking up stitches through edges of both pieces at same time to join, *work Attached I-cord to 1 stitch before top of point, work 1 row Unattached I-cord, work [1 row Attached I-cord, 2 rows Unattached I-cord, 1 row Attached I-cord] all in stitch at top of

point, work 1 row Unattached I-cord, work Attached I-cord down to base of point; repeat from* 7 times more, stuffing a small amount of fiberfill into sun before completing last point. Join ends of I-cord.

BAG

Make 2 squares and 1 sun. Sew face buttons on sun. Sew sun in center of one square, sewing around sun center and leaving triangle points unsewn. Stuff sun with a small amount of fiberfill before closing. Tack down ends of points.

Join squares with I-cord edging and make strap

With dpns and A, cast on 3 stitches. With RS of square with sun facing, begin at top right corner and work Attached I-cord along top edge to next corner, then with WS of both squares together, and picking up stitches through both pieces at same time to join, *work [1 row Attached I-cord, 1 row Unattached I-cord, 1 row Attached I-cord] all in corner stitch, work Attached I-cord to next corner; repeat from* twice more, then pick up and knit 1 stitch in corner stitch—4 stitches.

Next row Slide stitches to opposite end of needle, k4.

Next row Slide stitches, k2, M1, k2—5 stitches.

***Next row** Slide stitches, k5; repeat from* until strap measures 28".

Next row Slide stitches, k2, k2tog, k1—4 stitches.

Next row Slide stitches, k2, k2tog—3

BARUFFA Merinos Otto (wool; 50g; 99 yds) in 26733 yellow, 1254 red, and 27160 blue, colors used as desired

stitches. Work Attached I-cord along top edge of back Square. Join I-cord ends.

PILLOW
Make 2 squares and 1 sun. Sew face buttons on sun. Attach sun to square same as for bag. With WS of both squares together, work Attached I-cord with A around edges of pillow as for joined sides of bag, working through both pieces at once. Stuff pillow with fiberfill before closing.

TECHNIQUES INDEX

CABLE CAST-ON

1 Start with a slipknot on left needle (first cast-on stitch). Insert right needle into slipknot from front. Wrap yarn over right needle as if to knit.

2 Bring yarn through slipknot, forming a loop on right needle.
3 Insert left needle in loop and slip loop off right needle. One additional stitch cast on.

4 Insert right needle **between** the last 2 stitches. From this position, knit a stitch and slip it to the left needle as in Step 3. Repeat Step 4 for each additional stitch.

CROCHET CAST-ON

1 Leaving a short tail, make a slipknot on crochet hook. Hold hook in right hand; in left hand, hold knitting needle on top of yarn and behind hook. With hook to left of yarn, bring yarn through loop on hook; yarn goes over top of needle, forming a stitch.

2 Bring yarn under point of needle and hook yarn through loop forming next stitch. Repeat Step 2 until 1 stitch remains to cast on. Slip loop from hook to needle for last stitch.

LOOP CAST-ON (ALSO CALLED E-WRAP CAST-ON)

Left-slanting   *Right-slanting*

Often used to cast on a few stitches, as for a buttonhole
1 Hold needle and tail in left hand.
2 Bring right index finger under yarn, pointing toward you.

3 Turn index finger to point away from you.
4 Insert tip of needle under yarn on index finger (see above); remove finger and draw yarn snug, forming a stitch. Repeat Steps 2–4 until all stitches are on needle.

Loops can be formed over index or thumb and can slant to the left or to the right. On the next row, work through back loop of right-slanting loops

TUBULAR CAST-ON

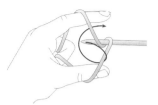

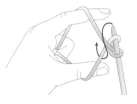

1 Leaving a tail approximately 4 times the width of the cast-on, fold the yarn over needle. Bring yarn between fingers of left hand and wrap around little finger as shown.

2 Bring left thumb and index finger between strands, arranging so tail is on thumb side. Open thumb and finger so strands form a diamond. Take needle **over index yarn, then under it.**

3 Bring needle **over thumb yarn** then **under it and under index yarn,** forming a purl stitch on needle.

4 Bring needle toward you, **over thumb yarn, under it,** and up between the two yarns.

5 Bring needle **over and under** the **index yarn.** Bring index yarn **under thumb yarn,** forming a knit stitch on the needle.

6 Take needle over index yarn, then under it. Repeat Steps 3–6.

7 End with Step 3. Note that knit stitches alternate with purl stitches.

LIFTED INCREASE, KNIT OR PURL

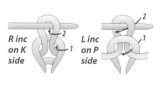

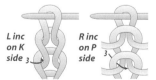

Work increase before stitch
Knit or purl into right loop of stitch in row below next stitch on left needle (1), then knit or purl into stitch on needle (2).

Work increase after stitch
Knit or purl next stitch on left needle, then knit or purl into left loop of stitch in row below this stitch (3).

ABBREVIATIONS

CC contrasting color
cn cable needle
cm centimeter(s)
dec decreas(e)(ed)(es)(ing)
dpn double-pointed needle(s)
g gram(s)
" inch(es)
inc increas(e)(ed)(es)(ing)
k knit(ting)(s)(ted)
LH left-hand

M1 Make one stitch (increase)
m meter(s)
mm millimeter(s)
MC main color
oz ounce(s)
p purl(ed)(ing)(s) or page
pm place marker
psso pass slipped stitch(es) over
RH right-hand
RS right side(s)
sc single crochet
sl slip(ped)(ping)
SKP slip, knit, psso
SSK slip, slip, knit these 2 sts tog
SSP slip, slip, purl these 2 sts tog
st(s) stitch(es)
St st stockinette stitch
tbl through back of loop(s)
WS wrong side(s)
wyib with yarn in back
wyif with yarn in front
yd(s) yard(s)
YO(2) yarn over (twice)

S2KP2, sl 2-k1-p2sso

1 Slip 2 stitches **together** to right needle as if to knit.

2 Knit next stitch.

3 Pass 2 slipped stitches over knit stitch and off right needle: 3 stitches become 1; the center stitch is on top.

4 The result is a centered double decrease.

SLIP KNITWISE (sl 1 k-wise)

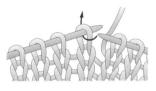

1 Insert right needle into next stitch on left needle from front to back (as if to knit).

2 Slide stitch from left to right needle. Stitch orientation changes (right leg of stitch loop is at back of needle).

SLIP PURLWISE (sl 1 p-wise)

1 Insert right needle into next stitch on left needle from back to front (as if to purl).

2 Slide stitch from left to right needle. Stitch orientation does not change (right leg of stitch loop is at front of needle).

MAKE 1 LEFT (M1L), KNIT

1 Insert left needle from front to back under strand between last stitch knitted and first stitch on left needle. Knit, twisting strand by working into loop at back of needle.

2 Completed M1L knit: a left-slanting increase.

MAKE 1 RIGHT (M1R), KNIT

1 Insert left needle from back to front under strand between last stitch knitted and first stitch on left needle. Knit, twisting the strand by working into loop at front of the needle.

2 Completed M1R knit: a right-slanting increase.

82

3-NEEDLE BIND-OFF

Bind-off ridge on wrong side
1 With stitches on 2 needles, place **right sides together**. * Knit 2 stitches together (1 from front needle and 1 from back needle); repeat from * once more (as shown).
2 With left needle, pass first stitch on right needle over second stitch and off right needle.

3 Knit next 2 stitches together.
4 Repeat Step 2.
5 Repeat Steps 3 and 4, end by drawing yarn through last stitch.

Bind-off ridge on right side
Work as for ridge on wrong side, EXCEPT, with **wrong sides together**.

SSK

1 Slip 2 stitches **separately** to right needle as if to knit.

2 Slip left needle into these 2 stitches from left to right and knit them together: 2 stitches become 1.

The result is a left-slanting decrease.

INTARSIA - PICTURE KNITTING

Color worked in areas of stockinette fabric: each area is made with its own length of yarn. Twists made at each color change connect these areas.

TIPS
• Intarsia blocks are always worked back and forth, even in circular work.
• When bobbins are called for, make a butterfly or cut 3-yard lengths to prevent tangles.
• Work across a row and back before you untangle yarns.

Right-side row　　　　　**Wrong-side row**

Making a twist:
Work across row to color change, pick up new color from under the old and work across to next color change.

GRAFT IN STOCKINETTE

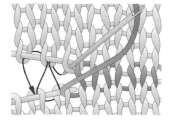

1 Arrange stitches on 2 needles as shown.
2 Thread a blunt needle with matching yarn (approximately 1" per stitch).
3 Working from right to left, with right sides facing you, begin with Steps 3a and 3b:
3a Front needle: bring yarn through first stitch **as if to purl**, leave stitch **on needle.**
3b Back needle: bring yarn through first stitch **as if to knit**, leave stitch **on needle.**
4a Front needle: bring yarn through first stitch **as if to knit**, **slip off** needle; through next stitch **as if to purl**, leave stitch **on needle.**
4b Back needle: bring yarn through first stitch **as if to purl**, **slip off** needle; through next stitch **as if to knit**, leave stitch **on needle.**
Repeat Steps 4a and 4b until 1 stitch remains on each needle.
5a Front needle: bring yarn through stitch **as if to knit**, slip **off needle.**
5b Back needle: bring yarn through stitch **as if to purl**, slip **off needle.**
6 Adjust tension to match rest of knitting.

YARN OVER (YO)

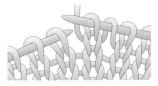

Between knit stitches
Bring yarn under needle to the front, take it over the needle to the back and knit the next stitch.

Completed yo increase.

After a knit, before a purl
Bring yarn under the needle to the front, over the needle to the back, then under the needle to the front; purl next stitch.

After a purl, before a knit
With yarn in front of the needle, bring it over the needle to the back; knit next stitch.

KNIT IN ROUNDS

• After casting on, do not turn work. Knit into first cast-on stitch to join. Stop. Check to make sure that the cast-on does not spiral around the needle. If it does, undo the stitch, remove the spiral, then rejoin.

• Check your knitting at end of first and second rounds and make sure you have no twists.

• Mark the beginning of a round in one of three ways:

1 Place a marker on needle.

2 Use a safety pin in the fabric.

3 Weave your leftover cast-on tail between first and last stitch of round.

WORK WITH 3 DOUBLE-POINTED NEEDLES (DPNS)

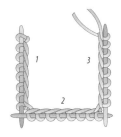

Cast stitches onto 1 dpn.
1 Rearrange stitches on 3 dpns. Check carefully that stitches are not twisted around a dpn or between dpns before beginning to work in rounds.

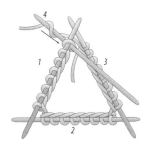

2 With a 4th dpn, work all stitches from first dpn. Use that empty dpn to work the stitches from the 2nd dpn. Use that empty dpn to work the stitches from the 3rd dpn—one round completed. Place a marker between first and second

stitch of first needle to mark beginning of round.
Notice that you work with only 2 dpns at a time. As you work the first few rounds, be careful that th stitches do not twist between the needles.

PICK UP STITCHES IN A CHAIN

A temporary cast-on
1 With crochet hook and waste yarn, loosely chain the number of stitches needed, plus a few extra chains. Cut yarn.

2 With needle and main yarn, pick up and knit 1 stitch into the back 'purl bump' of the first chain. Continue, knitting 1 stitch into each chain until you have the required number of stitches. Do not work into remaining chains.

CROCHET CHAIN STITCH (ch st, ch)

1 Make a slipknot to begin.
2 Catch yarn and draw through loop on hook.

First chain made. Repeat Step 2.

84

POMPONS

1 Cut 2 pieces of cardboard half the desired width of the pompon.
2 Place a length of yarn between cardboard pieces.
3 Hold the pieces together and wrap yarn around them.

4 Tie the length of yarn tightly at one edge.
5 Cut the wrapped yarn on opposite side.

6 Remove cardboard, fluff, and trim pompon.
7 Use ties to attach.

DUPLICATE STITCH

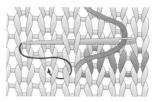

With a blunt tapestry needle threaded with a length of yarn of a contrasting color, cover a knitted stitch with an embroidered stitch.

TASSELS

1 Wrap yarn around a piece of cardboard that is the desired length of the tassel. Thread a strand of yarn under the wraps, and tie it at the top, leaving a long end.

2 Cut the wrapped yarn at lower edge. Wrap the long end of yarn around upper edge and thread the yarn through the top as shown. Trim strands.

ATTACHED I-CORD

1 With double-pointed needle, cast on 3 or 4 sts, then pick up and knit 1 stitch along edge of piece—4 or 5 stitches.

2 Slide stitches to opposite end of dpn and k2 or k3, then k2tog through the back loops, pick up and knit 1 stitch from edge. Repeat Step 2 for I-cord.

UNATTACHED I-CORD

Make a tiny tube of stockinette stitch with 2 double-pointed needles:
1 Cast on 3 or 4 stitches.
2 Knit. Do not turn work. Slide stitches to opposite end of needle. Repeat Step 2 until cord is the desired length.

SSP

Use instead of p2tog-tbl to avoid twisting the stitches.

1 Slip 2 stitches **separately** to right needle as if to knit.

2 Slip these 2 stitches back onto left needle. Insert right needle through their 'back loops,' into the second stitch and then the first.

3 Purl them together: 2 stitches become 1.

The result is a left-slanting decrease.

85

Pattern Specifications

INTERMEDIATE One size Circumference 19"	▸ *Skill level* *Size* *and measurements*
 10cm/4" 27 ▦ 21 • over stockinette stitch (knit on RS, purl on WS)	▸ *Gauge* *The number of stitches and* *rows you need in 10 cm or* *4", worked as specified.*
1 2 3 5 6 • Medium weight MC, A, B, C, D, E, F • 88 yds each	▸ *Yarn weight* *and amount in yards*
• four 4.5mm/US7 double-pointed needles (dpn), or size to obtain gauge • 4.5mm/US7 40cm/16" long	▸ *Type of needles* *Straight, unless circular* *or double-pointed* *are recommended.*
& • stitch marker • yarn needle	▸ *Any extras*

86

Measuring

- **A** Bust/Chest
- **B** Body length
- **C** Center back to cuff
  (arm slightly bent)

Fit

STANDARD FIT
bust/chest
plus 2–4"

LOOSE FIT
bust/chest
plus 4–6"

OVERSIZED FIT
bust/chest
plus 6" or more

Sizing

Measure around the fullest part of your bust/chest to find your size.

Children	2	4	6	8	10	12	14
Actual chest	21"	23"	25"	26½"	28"	30"	31½"

At a Glance

Conversion chart

centimeters	0.394	inches
grams	0.035	ounces
inches	2.54	centimeters
ounces	28.6	grams
meters	1.1	yards
yards	.91	meters

Needles/Hooks

US	MM	HOOK
0	2	A
1	2.25	B
2	2.75	C
3	3.25	D
4	3.5	E
5	3.75	F
6	4	G
7	4.5	7
8	5	H
9	5.5	I
10	6	J
10½	6.5	K
11	8	L
13	9	M
15	10	N
17	12.75	

Equivalent weights

¾	oz	20 g
1	oz	28 g
1½	oz	40 g
1¾	oz	50 g
2	oz	60 g
3½	oz	100 g

Yarn weight categories

Yarn Weight

1	2	3	4	5	6
Super Fine	**Fine**	**Light**	**Medium**	**Bulky**	**Super Bulky**

Also called

Sock Fingering Baby	Sport Baby	DK Light-Worsted	Worsted Afghan Aran	Chunky Craft Rug	Bulky Roving

Stockinette Stitch Gauge Range 10cm/4 inches

27 sts to 32 sts	23 sts to 26 sts	21 sts to 24 sts	16 sts to 20 sts	12 sts to 15 sts	6 sts to 11 sts

Recommended needle (metric)

2.25 mm to 3.25 mm	3.25 mm to 3.75 mm	3.75 mm to 4.5 mm	4.5 mm to 5.5 mm	5.5 mm to 8 mm	8 mm and larger

Recommended needle (US)

1 to 3	3 to 5	5 to 7	7 to 9	9 to 11	11 and larger

Yarn substitutions

Throughout this book, the photo caption describes the yarns and colors in the photograph. If a yarn is not available, its yardage and content information will help in making a substitution. Locate the Yarn Weight and Stockinette Stitch Gauge Range over 10cm to 4" on the chart. Compare that range with the information on the yarn label to find an appropriate yarn. These are guidelines only for commonly used gauges and needle sizes in specific yarn categories.

Contributors

Kathy Cheifetz

Bonnie Franz

Julie Gaddy

Katharine Hunt

Megan Lacey

Rick Mondragon

Uschi Nolte

Celeste Pinheiro

Lois Young

Diane Zangl

Kathy Zimmerman